CRICUT DESIGN SPACE

vol. 2

THE GUIDE TO MASTERING ALL ASPECTS OF CRICUT DESIGN SPACE

Made with love

by

Sienna

Tally

TABLE OF CONTENTS

CHAPTER 3: HOW TO USE IMAGES 45

CHAPTER 4: CRICUT DESIGN SPACE TIPS AND TRICKS 56

Introduction

Welcome back readers with the second volume dedicated to virtual design through design space: "Cricut design space vol. 2 ".

Unlike the other guides I remind you that in order to understand everything that is written in this volume is necessary to have the basics for the use of Design Space, or, have read my previous guide "Cricut Design Space vol. 1 ".

Cricut is a machine that helps you in making designs and creating innumerable arts and crafts projects. It is such a hit among enthusiasts because it works on paper and can also create and cut designs for other materials like vinyl, cloth, cardboard, and more. You can even use it for wood!

Professional designers and artists mostly use it for their different projects. However, Cricut is becoming a household name through the sleek design's availability, where even young people can experiment to check their creative strengths. Through a Cricut machine, you can draw, emboss or deboss and then cut out your chosen design.

The best thing about this fantastic piece of technology is that its usage is pretty simple. It means that even if you have never used such a device before, or if you are new to the world of art, you can still learn to use the Cricut machine with some guidance.

And this is why Cricut Design Space is ideal. It helps users develop ideas, styles, drawings, and more to generate something unique and distinctly their own.

Cricut for Business

Have you been thinking of working from home and set up your own business? Have you always been into arts and crafts, clothing, or woodwork? Then Cricut machine can help you establish your very own business right from the comfort of your house. Through the use of Cricut Design Space, you can come up with beautiful, original designs that can then be used to start up your own business. Depending on what you wish to do, you can have your woodwork place, your boutique with cutwork clothes, and even an arts-and-crafts, Etsy-type store.

Your Cricut Design Space app will help you select designs that are already available and customize them to come up with something different that isn't already present in the market. It would become a kind of signature style that only your business promotes and sells.

Not sure how this can work out? Let's consider an example. So, you are into quilt designs. You have already worked on some, and everyone around you loves to have you gift them something. You know you have a talent but don't have the stamina or the strength to keep creating quilts after quilts. Meet your best friend, the Cricut machine that will make quilting a unique yet enjoyable experience for you. With a Cricut Maker's help, you can easily cut all shapes while using hundreds of fabrics. The accuracy and precision that you will obtain through this machine are going to throw you in awe. And the best part? Your work will be done at least in a triple faster time. You will not have to spend weeks on one quilt because your Cricut machine will get the job done in a few short days! If once you were only able to quilt one quilt a month, you will now create many. Just imagine the business you will have. Your passion will be making money for you!

And then once you have begun, there is no stopping you. With the help of social media, you can popularize your business venture in a short period and quickly make a name for yourself in the world of quiltmakers.

Of course, how big or small you wish to keep your business will be up to you. In some time, you may even be able to hire help to do extra work for you! Enticed? Think about it even more and remember, quilting is only one such business that your Cricut machine will help you start. There are many other options that you can choose from.

The only thing you will need to put your mind to is what you like doing and whether or not that venture will have any demand in your area. The whole point of a small-scale business or home-based business is that you pick a project you know is in order. So, get researching and find out what you can do with your skillful and innovative Cricut machine and your Cricut Design Space.

The Many Projects You Can Start with Cricut

A Cricut machine cuts stuff for you in all the shapes, sizes, and varieties you can think of. It means it is a crafter's dream come true, no matter what industry they belong to. If you are one such crafter, then here are all the things you can do with a Cricut machine.

1.   Creating Cards

One of the most straightforward and essential things you can do with a Cricut machine is creating cards. You can cut out any shape of any size and either stick it on cards or even cut your card design in a specific manner. With the help of your Cricut Design Space, you can cut and flip shapes to create a unique design and weld together different formats into one whole. You can even align lines to precision, arrange various elements to see how they would go together, rotate shapes to fit them correctly and try different fonts and sizes. Most importantly, you can attach all the things to cut in just the right manner.

Depending on what kind of cards you want to create, you can decide the color combination and the shape. The machine and Cricut Design Space app's whole point is to explore as many options as you can think of. The app allows you to visualize what you would otherwise only have had in your head.

2.   Vinyl Projects

Vinyl is another thing that you can use for your Cricut projects. Vinyl is a kind of plastic used for multiple items, from food labels to crayon holders, stencils, and more. With the aid of a Cricut machine, you can easily create various designs for pretty much everything you can think of. But what is even better is that the Design Space app will help you believe first out through virtual design to figure out if it is even possible to come up with a product that you have imagined in your head. Be it shapes, sizes, or cuts, you can either choose them from the samples given, or you can come up with your signature style.

Of course, you will have to find out which type of vinyl is best for what kind of product. So do your research before beginning any project.

3.   Home Décor

Just the thought of home décor sends some people into rapturous reviews, while others would only groan at the idea. If you fall into the former category, then Cricut is your new best buddy. Why? Because you can design multiple objects with this machine and its perfect app. From spice baskets to children's toys, wall art, to hanging plant holders, you think it, and the device can do it for you. You can even come up with unique designs that are distinctly your own. People would be mesmerized by what you can do with your imagination.

These DIY home décor items will be projects to opt for all the rooms in your house and outside the house. You can easily create your door wreaths, planters, even fake plants if that is what you wish!

The great thing about these DIY projects is that they are one of a kind that no one else can make. You can even make gifts for your loved ones or the dear ones who love personalized presents. Imagine how people will love the effort you put in, giving them something to remember you by.

4.   Jewelry

It's another thing that you can do with Cricut. Jewelry making is a fine art, and not everyone had the talent to come up with beautiful designs. With Cricut design space, you can bring to screen what you have in your mind's eye.

The perfect thing about using Cricut is that you can engage the entire family in this process. If your young ones have an interest in creative projects, then this is something they will enjoy immensely. Since a Cricut machine can be used for various materials, you can easily make artificial jewelry with it.

You can opt for different materials like wood, plastic, rubber, stone, gemstone, resin, and even vinyl for your jewelry projects. Just make sure that you do not allow very young children to handle it when it comes to the machine's actual usage. Even older kids will need some guidance from you. But as far as the use of design space is concerned, everyone who understands it can use it without supervision. Jewelry making was never as simple as it is with a Cricut machine.

5.   Woodwork

It is another handy creative work that you can enjoy alone, with family or even friends. The best part is that you cannot just make things with wood for your pleasure but also sell it and establish your venture. Keep in mind that a Cricut maker can cut materials that are less than 2.4 mm thick. It would help if you also had a new knife blade that is sharper and thicker for wood cutting, and you would have to purchase it separately.

When it comes to the type of woods for Cricut maker, basswood and balsa wood are ideal because they have a smooth texture that is easy to cut. What's more, the finishing that you can obtain with these woods is incomparable to any other. This is why most people who use Cricut maker for woodwork opt for these types of wood.

One more tip for woodwork is to make sure that you mark the wood with tapes while cutting to don't end up with wood with irregular cuttings. You can make frames, figurines, jewelry, ornaments, and even puzzle toys for kids! Design Space helps you make sure that all the pieces are perfectly aligned to one another by giving you the precision of design and cut.

6.   Holiday Items

Once you have a Cricut Maker, you can pretty much stop buying gifts from shops because you now can make them on your own. You can make your cards or personalized gifts like quilts, jewelry, décor items, and even acrylic items for birthdays. If you want to make it even more personal, create a kind of gift with their vinyl name on it! Imagine the look of pleasure when you present your mom or dad, for example, with a birthday rug that says "best Mom/Dad" that you made yourself! They will be over the moon!

But birthdays aren't the only occasions that can be blessed with your Cricut machine. You can make Christmas gifts, Easter eggs/surprises, Halloween decorations, as well as costumes with your Cricut machine. Did you know that you can even carve your pumpkin with a Cricut machine? Yes, life does become more fun when introducing the Cricut machine and Design Space to your family and friends.

And that's not it; you can even make your holiday decoration items, like ornaments, for Christmas. From the angel at the top to Halloween toppers for your food corner, you can pretty much come up with any holiday decoration. You can go as far as your imagination can take you.

There is so much that you can do without having to spend hundreds of dollars during the holiday season!

7.   Clothing

Clothing is another thing that the Cricut machine and Design Space can be used for. There are so many sample options that you can choose from, mix and match them, and come up with your unique style. From ordinary day clothes, special occasion costumes, to clothes for your loved ones, you can make whatever you envision.

But clothes aren't the only thing you can create. Anything made of fabric can easily be cut with a Cricut machine or designed on the Design app. Pillow cushions, throw rugs, curtains, doilies, rugs, blankets, quilts, you can decorate and create anything that you want. Sky seriously is the limit when it comes to the Cricut machine. Want to do patchwork? Cricut is there to save you hours of the day by cutting up patches in any size, all the same, as frequently, and as quickly as you want.

If you like sewing and making your clothes, you can also present them to your loved ones. If not, you can always customize blank tees, jackets, and jeans with your Cricut design space.

Customizing clothing and fabric had never been more comfortable.

8.   3-D Projects

Ever been fascinated by the idea of 3-D projects? If you have the circuit machine and Design Space, then it is something that you can try for yourself. You can make your paper toys, gift boxes, and your wood items, as mentioned above.

Cricut is also ideal for professional architects and designers because they understand the need for and importance of 3-D designs. You can quickly draw on the screen what you wish to make and then bring it to reality through your Cricut machine. The best part? Unlike doing things with hands, it will not take you ages; you can do it within a few short minutes. What's more, the results are going to be precise like you may never have envisioned before. Now that you know about the actual machine, what it can do, and who it is best suited for, let's now figure out how you can take maximum benefit from it through the application of Cricut Design Space.

Chapter 1
SVG Files

WHAT ARE SVG FILES?

SVG Files is a file format for storing rich graphics. It is ultimately vector-based and can be scaled to any dimension without losing detail.

SVG files are an XML document that use several tags inside the <svg> tag to describe different elements.

Different tags are used for different shapes, such as circles, rectangles, ellipses, etc. Some elements act as containers for other elements or group sets of elements into a single element like <g>.

You can also add animation and interactivity with SVG files using SMIL.

SVG FILES AND CRICUT DESIGN SPACE

You can use SVG Files in Cricut Design Space by downloading SVG Files from your computer, uploading them into the SVG file gallery,

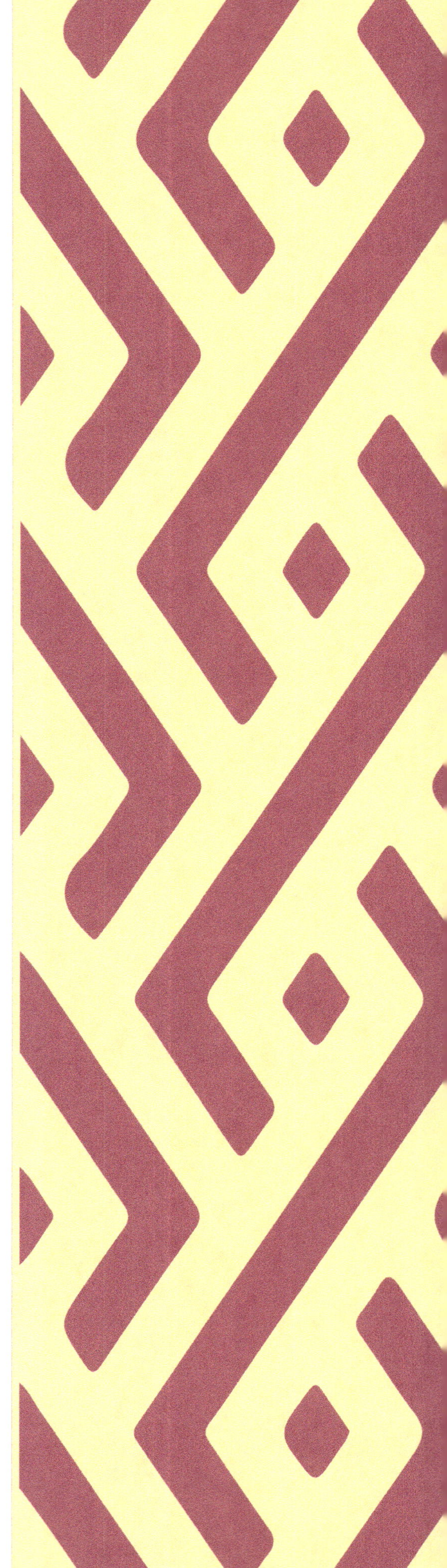

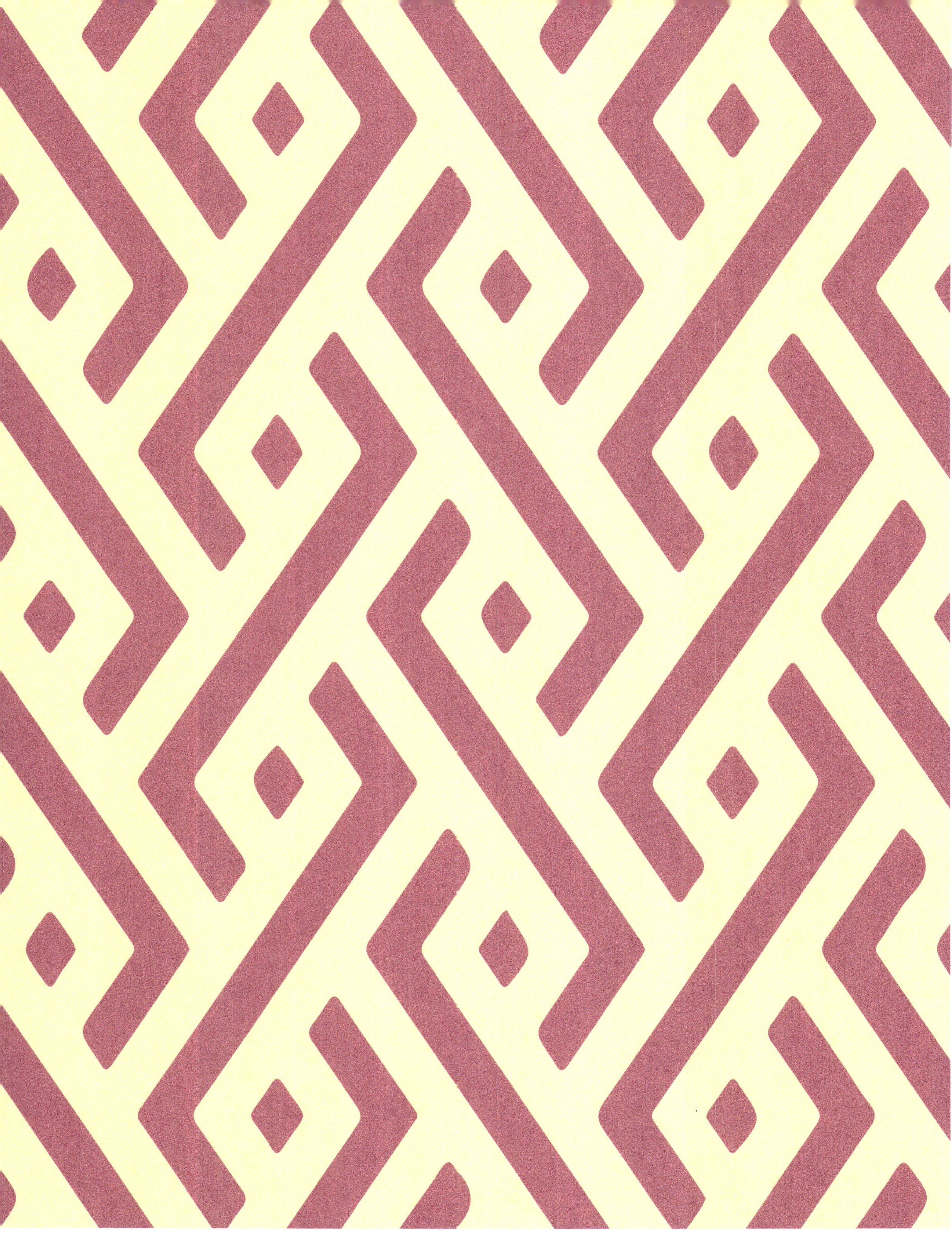

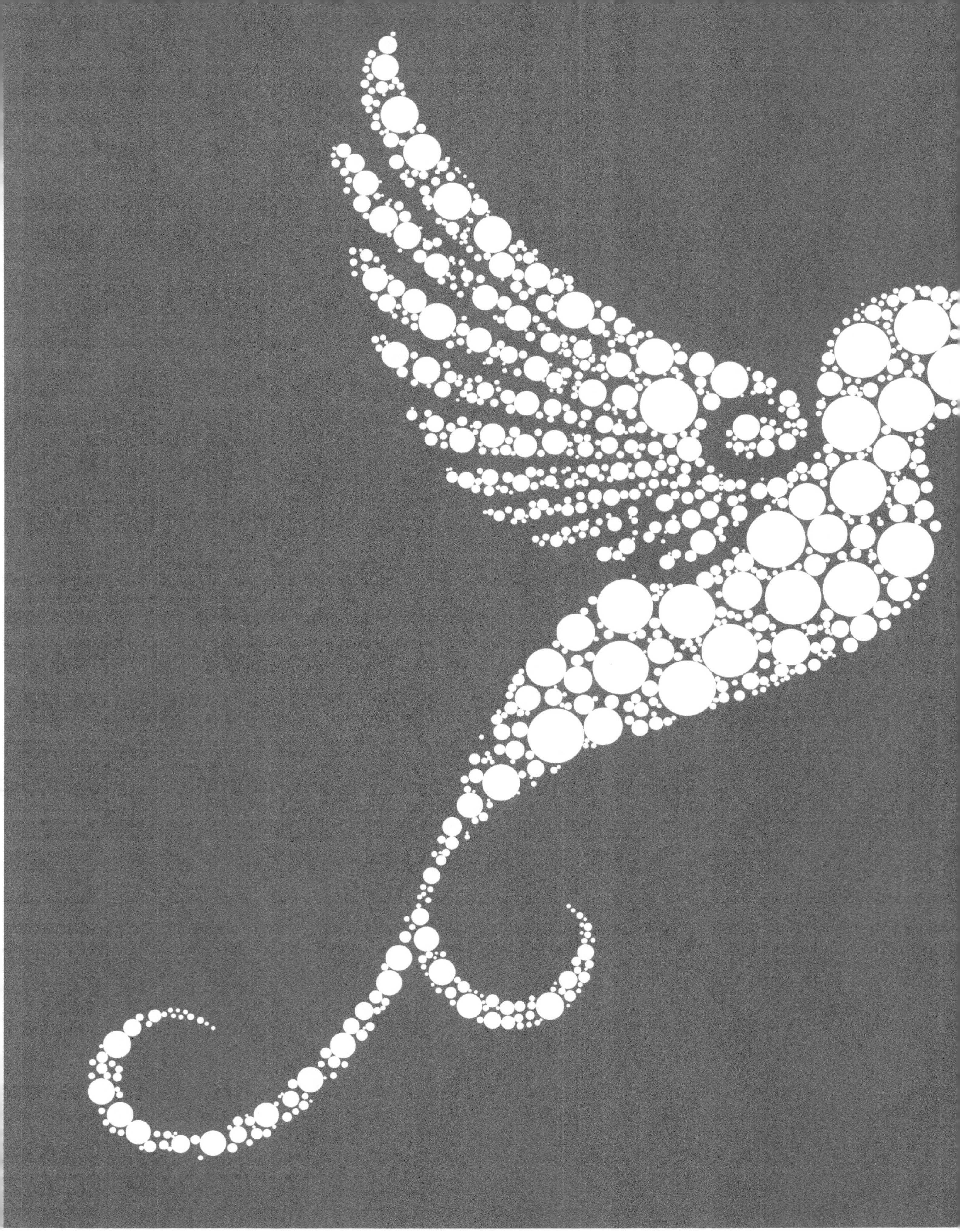

or Dropbox or Google Drive.

Inside Cricut Design Space, you can either use them in an SVG project or add them as a graphic to cut with your mat (just like a photo).

HOW TO CREATE SVG FILES

SVG files are vector image files. They are created in programs such as Adobe Illustrator and Inkscape.

In those programs, you can draw shapes using either line or fills, then group them to create a compound shape. Once done, you can export the file as an SVG image.

SVG IMAGE SIZES AND RESOLUTION

Most SVG images come in sizes of 1000 x 1000 pixels and 1500 x 1500 pixels. These images will get scaled-down when using them as a curable graphic on your mat (180 dpi) so that they look right when cutting on the Cricut machine. The larger this image is, the higher resolution (pixels per inch) it will need, meaning that it will take longer to print than a low-resolution image.

Image sizes are also dependent on the type of SVG file you create, whether it's a vector image or a bitmap image.

When creating a Graphic for Cricut cut files, you'll need to make sure that your graphic is high resolution and at least 1000 x 1000 pixels. If you're using an SVG file with a higher resolution, it can be scaled down to 180 dpi, which can be done by converting it into a PNG or JPG.

SVG FILES AND CRICUT CUT FILES: CREATION VS. SAVING

To understand how to use SVG with Cricut Design Space, we must first understand the difference between SVG cut files and SVG graphic files. If you save your SVG file as a normal Graphic (.jpg,.png,.gif), the design space machine will not recognize it as an SVG file. So how can this be? The answer is because instead of saving the created file in a folder called "SVG", you must save them in folders called "cuts". This is where they get recognized correctly by Design Space as an SVGs file.

With Design Space, there are two options for creating SVGs for cutting: Using brushes or using

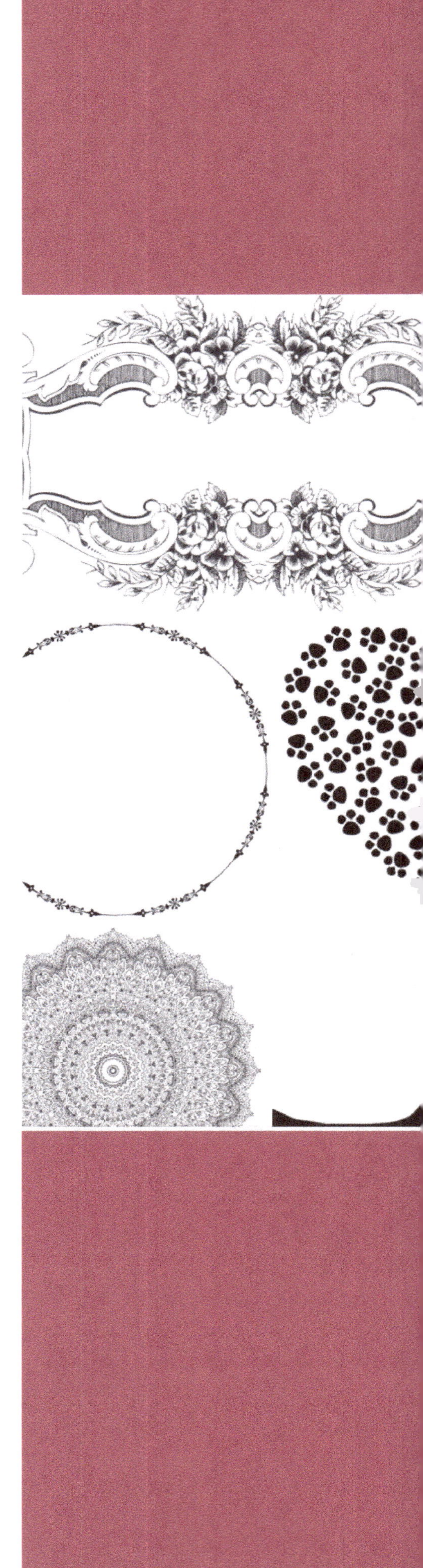

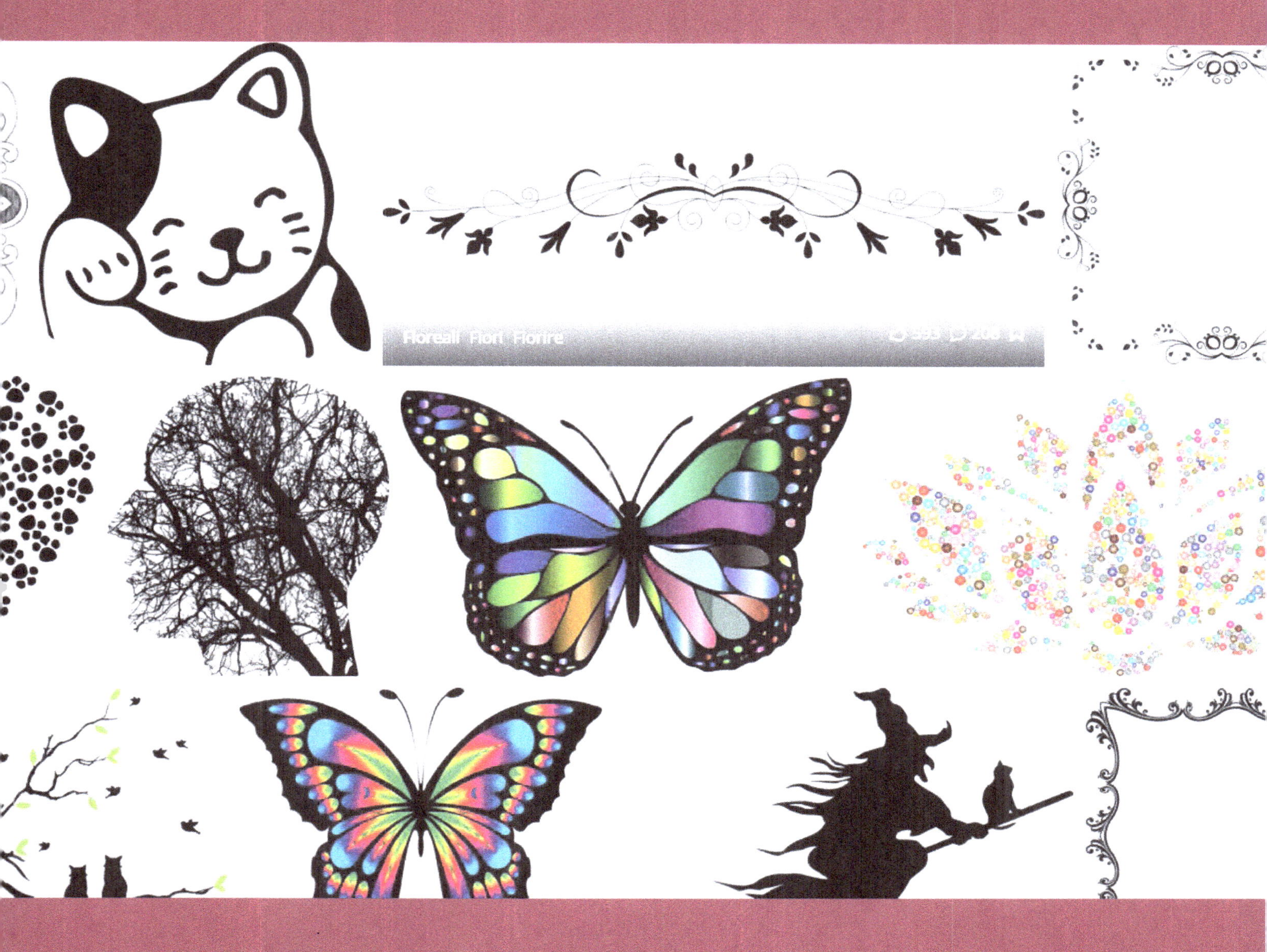
Floreali Fiori Fiorire

premade SVGs. With premade SVGs, you can save 10 SVGs in the same SVG file (separated by a semi-colon symbol). Your design space machine will recognize this as one graphic to cut, and all ten premade shapes will be cut simultaneously.

When exporting from Illustrator or Inkscape, your file must be saved in the "cuts" folder.

HOW TO CUT AN SVG FILE WITH CRICUT DESIGN SPACE

To use your SVG file with Design Space as a graphic on your mat, just follow these steps:

1. Upload your design (preferably vector) into the Cricut Design Space's SVG file gallery by clicking "Use Gallery". This puts your design in the gallery for easy access by other users of Design Space.

2. Upload any graphics you want to cut into CDS using either Design Space's tools or using the import/export button that appears when pressing ctrl+O.

3. In Design Space, select your SVG file or

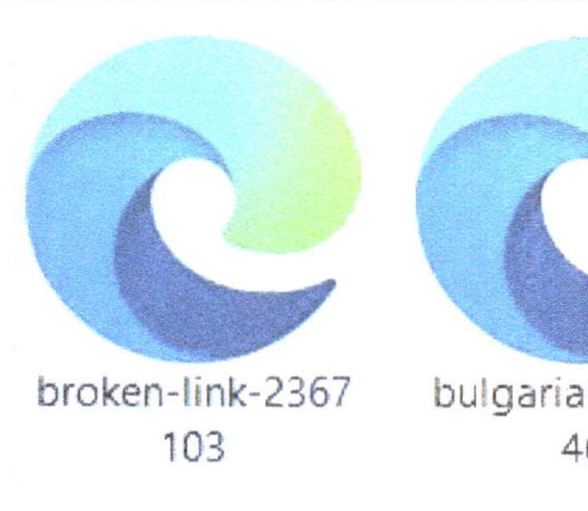

graphic and choose your mat.

When cutting, each cut will be placed in a separate file and saved into its folder.

SVG IMAGES FOR CRICUT PROJECTS

You can use SVG files with Cricut projects by uploading them into the gallery or dragging/dropping them into a project's image tab. If you drag/drop an image into the project tab, it will be pinned to the artboard's top-left corner. To move it around, un-pin them and then re-pin them where you want.

To add a graphic from your computer as an image in a project:

1. Open your Design Space project, click "Add" at the top of the window to open up the "add an element" box.

2. Locate "Use Files," then select Add Images and click OK. This will bring up your computer's file explorer, where you can search for whatever image you want on your computer to add to design space.) Click Add when you've selected the images you want to use in Design Space.

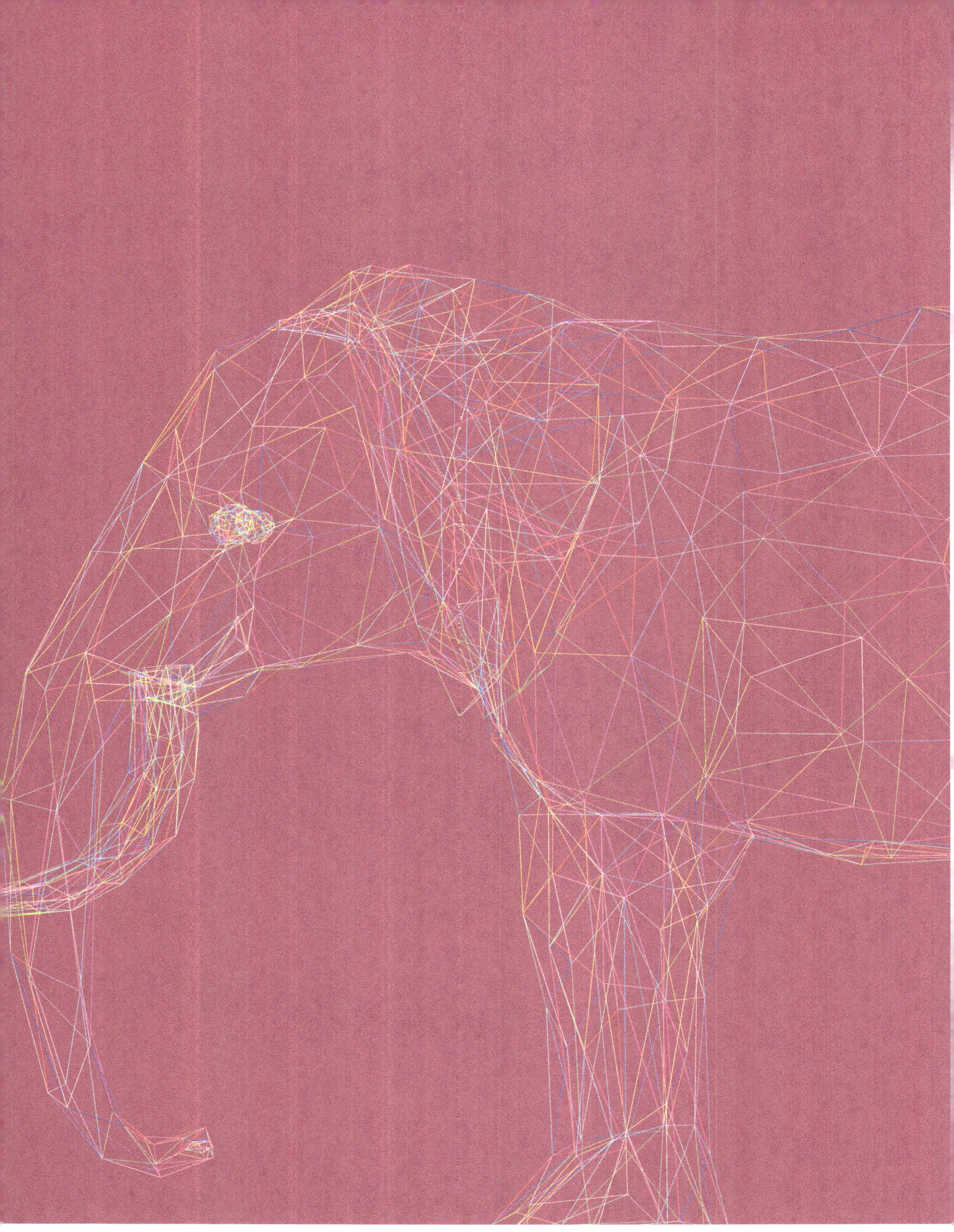

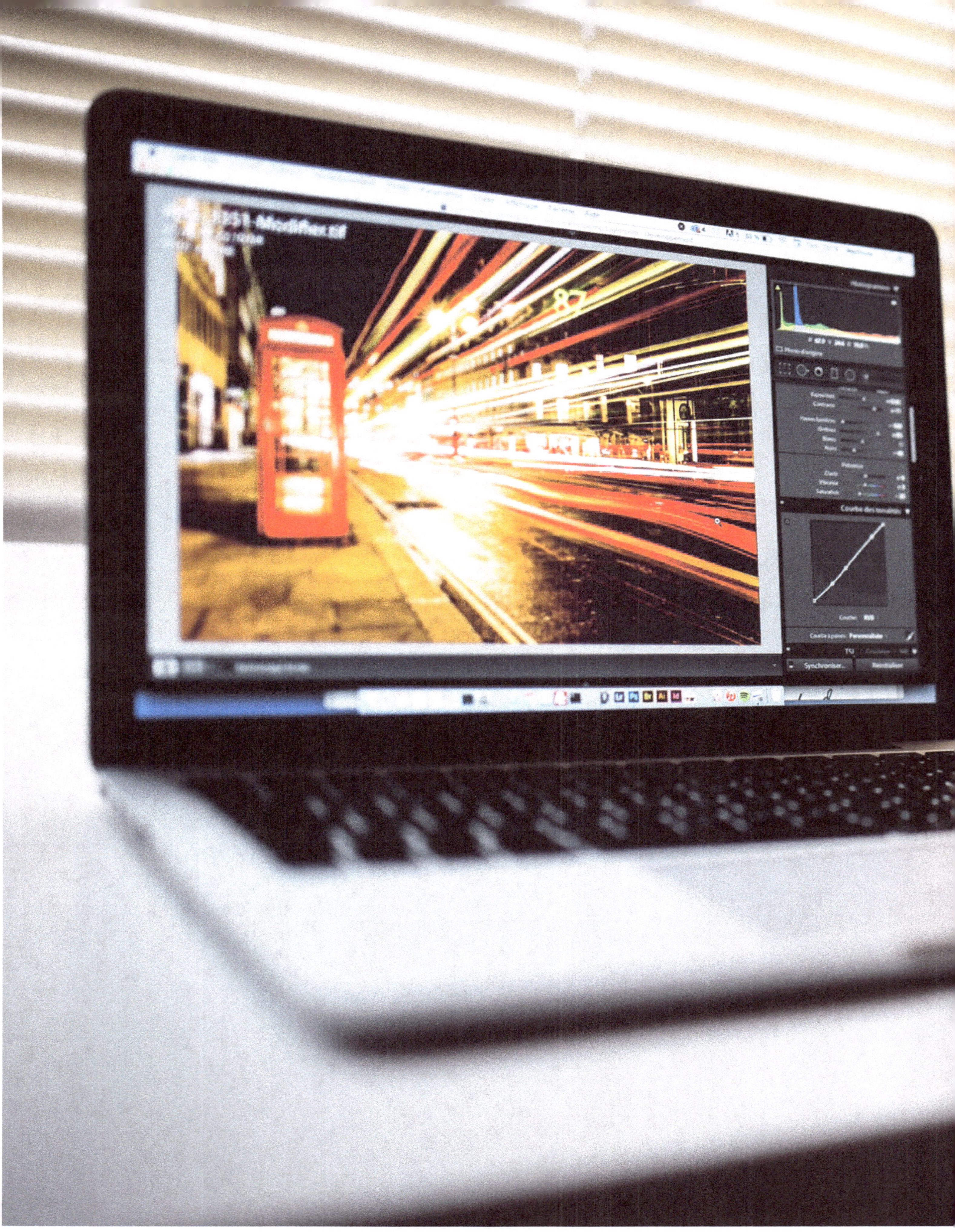

HOW TO EDIT SVG FILES

To edit an SVG file:

1. Go to the "Library" tab and select the SVG Files folder from the left-hand side of your screen. This will bring up all of the items in this gallery on the right-hand side of the screen, where you can click on any item to see its details by merging it with your library view (on the right).

2. Now double click on any item in the library view to open it (this action opens up a new browser window for viewing).

3. You can then edit the SVG file by opening it in your program that created it (i.e., Illustrator or Inkscape).

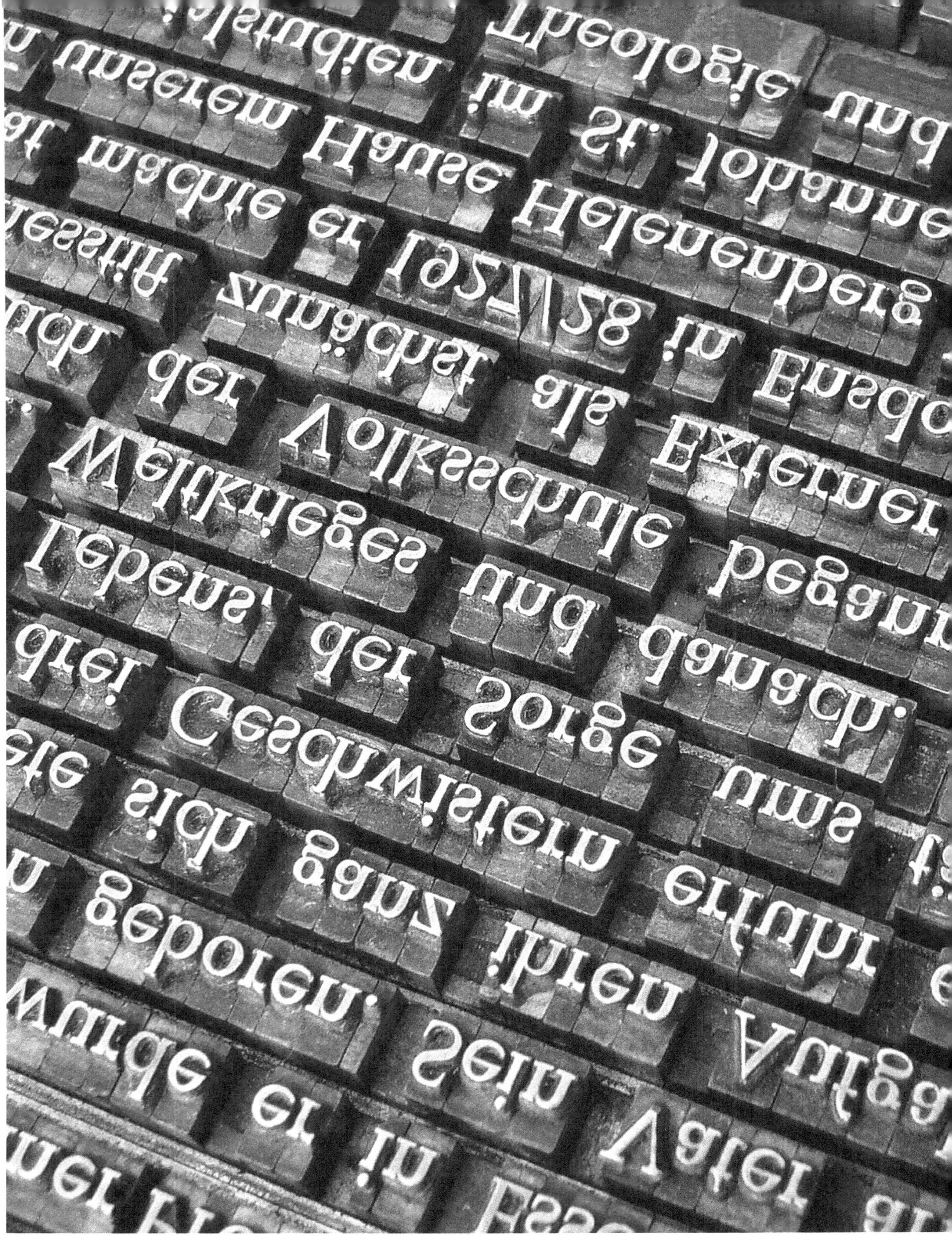

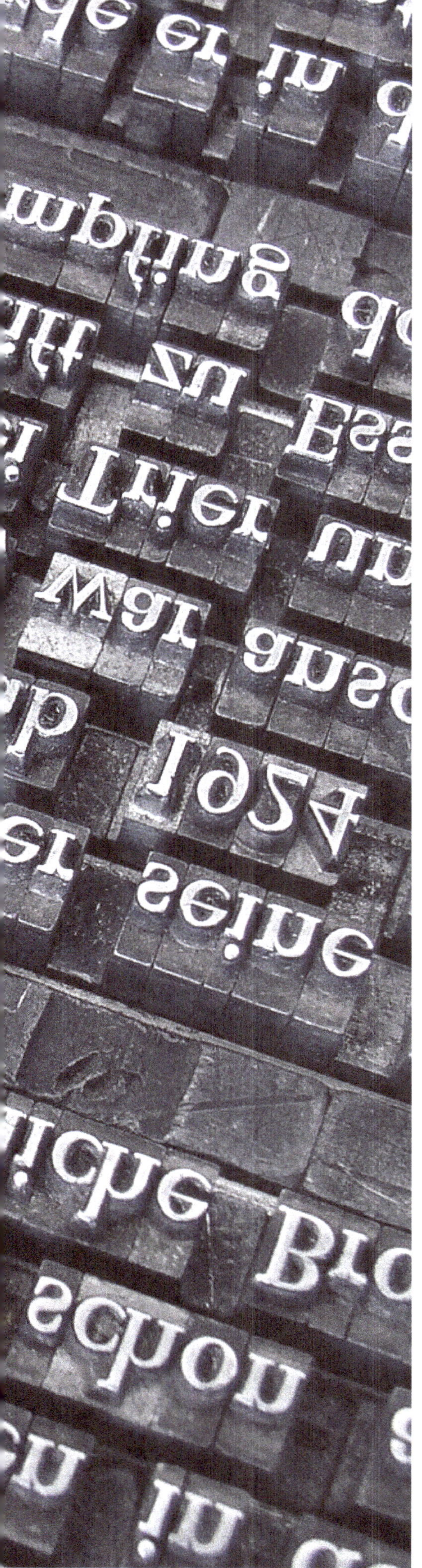

FINDING THAT PERFECT FONT

After you click that "Text" button on the Design Panel and type the text you're going to type into the textbox; it's time to choose what font you're going to use. We already talked about how to choose your font using the Text Edit Bar. I want to discuss the specifics.

CHOICES CHOICES

When you click on the dropdown menu under "Font" on the Text Edit Menu, you'll get a new bar like this:
This bar allows you to choose which font you want to use, which is pretty obvious. The thing that might not be as obvious as, "What do I do with these three options at the top - 'All,' 'System,' and 'Cricut?'"

Pressing "All" brings up every font available to be used in Cricut Design Space. Clicking "System" will show you only the fonts that are already downloaded on your PC. If you click "Cricut," Design Space will show you only the fonts that are available through Cricut Design Space.

FILTER

Because there are so many different types of fonts available through Cricut, they created a few simple ways to find the one you want. One way is by using the "Search Bar." This, of course, works for searching for your system's font as well as for a font in the Cricut system. The other way is through the "Filter" option. You'll see the clickable word, "Filter," to the right of the "Search" bar.

Under "Filter" is "My Fonts," "Multi-Layer," "Single-Layer," and "Writing." These groups are pretty self-explanatory.

"My Fonts" are fonts that you own. Yes, they are fonts on your system, yes, but they also include any fonts you uploaded to Cricut, fonts Cricut offers for free and fonts that you've already purchased.
"Multi-Layer" fonts are fonts that have more than one layer. If you were to use any multilayer fonts on your Canvas, they'd show up as two or more layers that could be separated and dealt with individually at will.

"Single Layer" fonts are fonts that show up as only one layer in your Layers Panel. "Single Layer" fonts and "Writing" fonts are the only fonts that can be sliced.

"Writing" fonts are the fonts that are specifically made for the Cricut to be able to write out instead of cutting out. Most of the Cricut fonts – and most

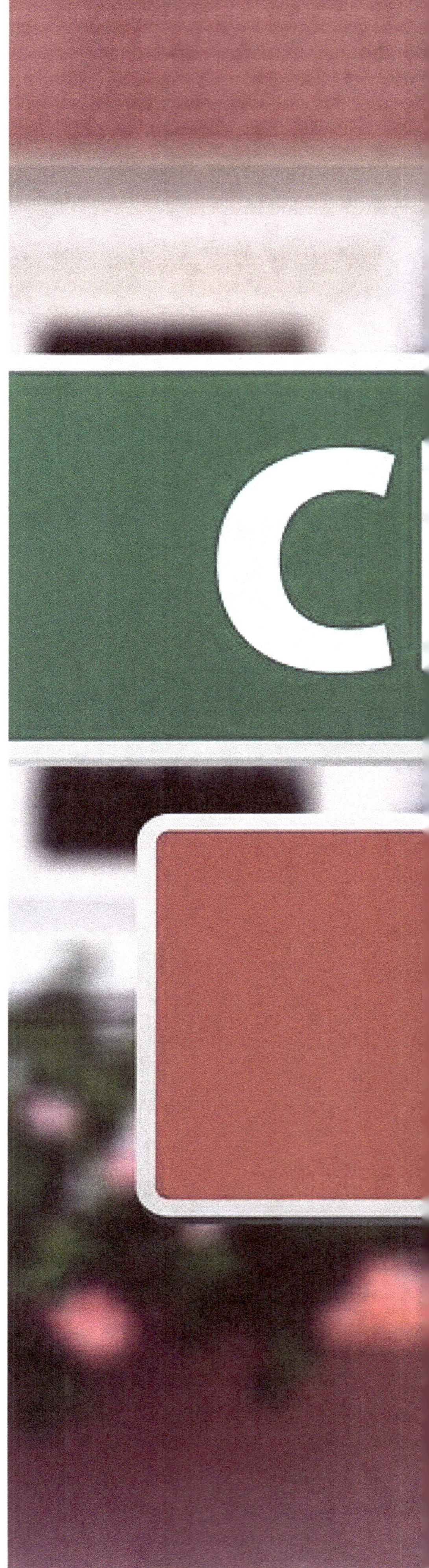

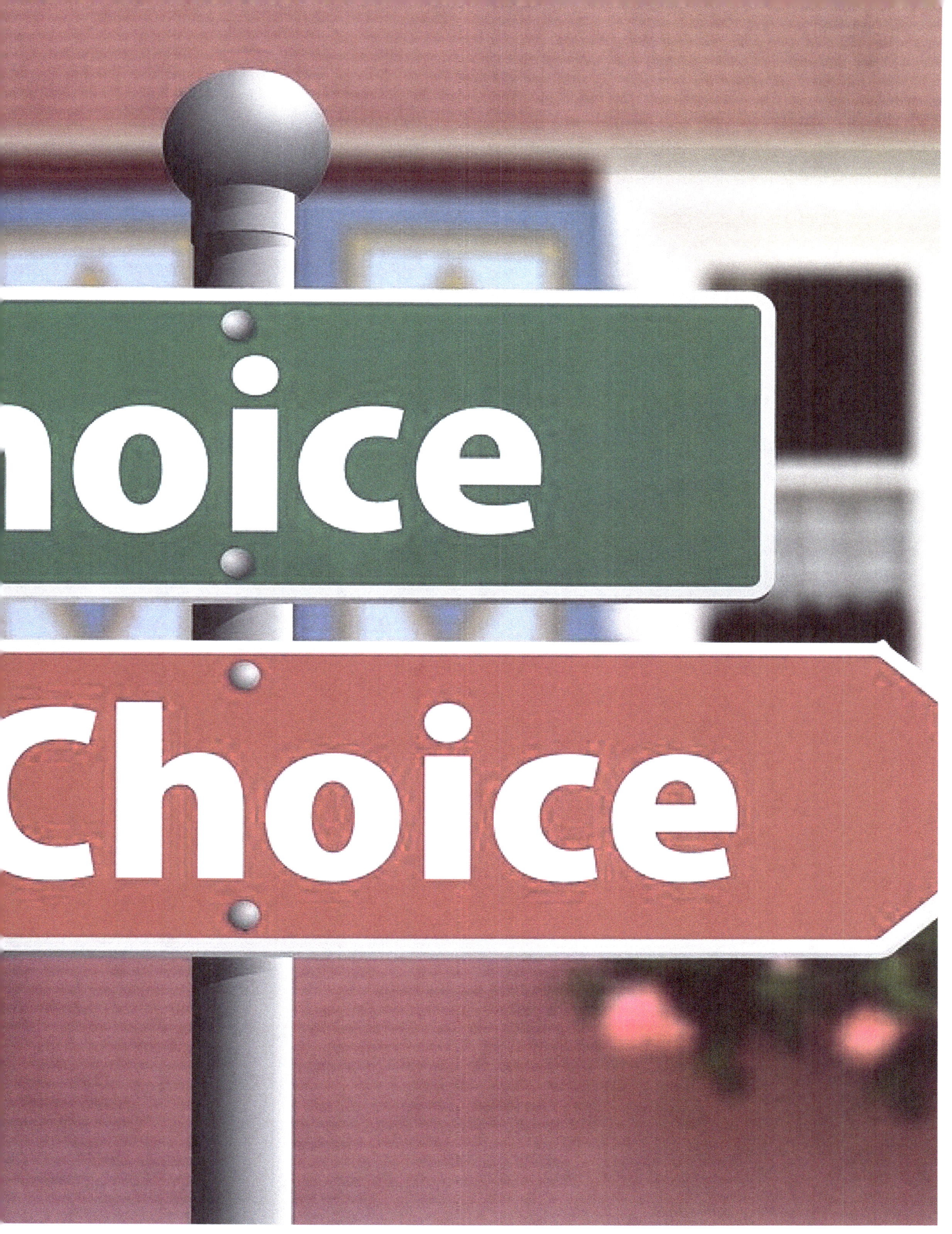

hoice
Choice

BLUEBERR

fonts-are made thick as far as that goes. Cricut fonts have to be thick so that they can be cut out. System fonts are often on the thicker side for good visibility.

Because of most fonts' thickness, Cricut was sure to designate a category for "Writing" fonts and even to create some anew. In the picture below, I included a Single Layered "Writing" font.

STYLE

Some "Multi-Layered" fonts can be easily made into "Writing" fonts with a click of the mouse. Others, however, do not have that option. Let me explain. If you look next door to "Font" on the Text Edit Bar, you'll see "Style." The drop-box there can be sneaky. It changes things up with every font. Some fonts have more styles available to them than others.

The possible styles are:
- Regular
- Bold
- Italic
- Bold Italic
- Writing
- Writing Italic

Some fonts can be manipulated more fully than others. Some cannot be italicized or made bold. In the same way, some fonts cannot be made into "Writing" fonts, but you'd be surprised at some of them that can be! Take the following for example:

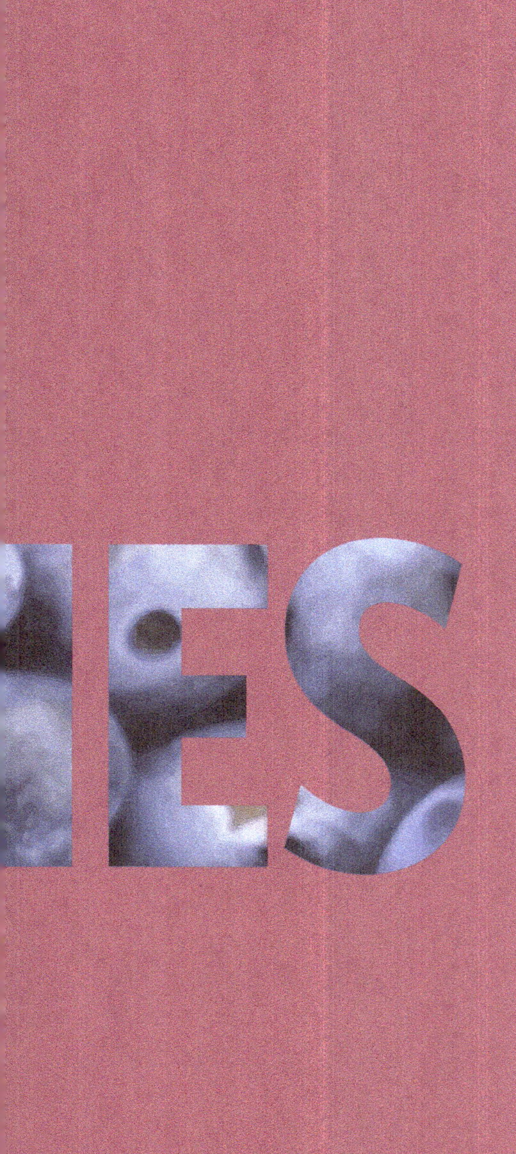

I think this is as right a place as any to throw this in. Remember that you can change your "Line" style too. This will also change the look of your font. Advanced Text Formatting Options

On the Text Edit Bar is another handy tool entitled

"ADVANCED." ADVANCED GIVES YOU THREE OPTIONS. THE TOOL'S OPTIONS ARE:

- Ungroup to Letters
- Ungroup to Lines
- Ungroup to Layers
- Ungroup to Letters

You can do so many neat things with your creations in Cricut Design Space when you know how to "Ungroup to Letters." It's a vital function to know about. We're going to talk about that now.

Using "Ungroup to Letters" is simple. You merely click on the text you want to manipulate, click "Advanced," and choose "Ungroup to Letters." This will allow you to move your letters around at will and whim freely.

This opens up many opportunities. If you can ungroup your letters, you can do all kinds of exciting things.

With ungrouping, you can also take letters in cursive fonts, which are naturally spaced further apart, and move them closer together. Once they touch, you can do your "Attach" or "Weld," as we saw above.

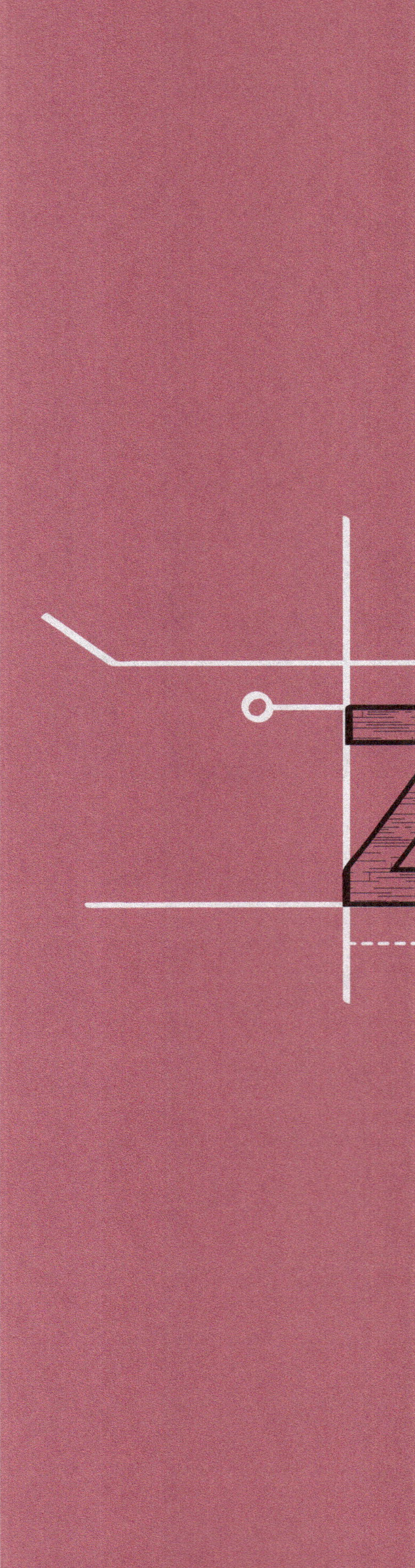

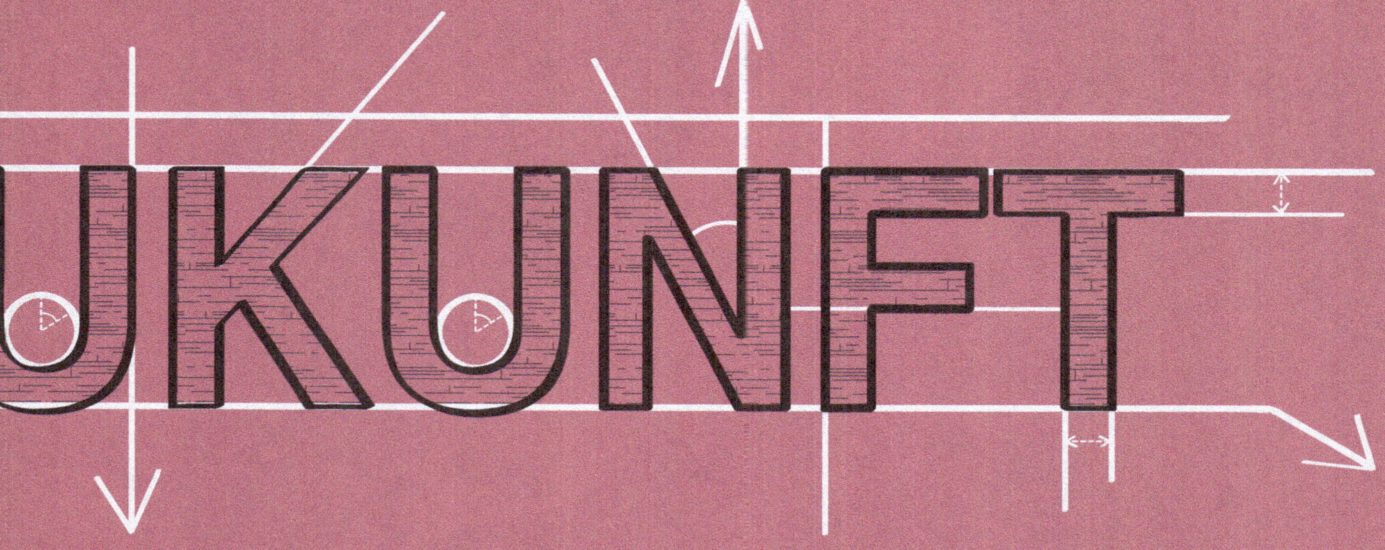
UKUNFT

Manually moving your letters is often necessary to making cursive fonts look right if you want them to touch. Moving them closer using only the "Letter Space" found on the Text Edit Bar will move each letter together by the same amount each time. Some letters are more comprehensive than others, so some letters end up touching long before others do. Therefore, if you merely keep spacing the letters closer together until they all touch, you end up with overlaps that look pretty bad.

UNGROUP TO LINES

If you want to type out several words in the same font but don't want them in a consecutive senten-ce, there's a quicker way to do that than starting a new textbox every time. Instead, start your text box line normal, but type your first word and press enter. Type your second word. Press enter again. Continue until you complete your sentence. Once you do, select your text, and click "Advanced." Then click "Ungroup to Lines."

When you choose to Ungroup your text into Lines, the word or words on each line will then be se-parated. You'll be able to freely move them to separate from the others until you regroup them.

UNGROUP TO LAYERS

Remember how I showed you how "Multi-Layer" fon-ts are added to your Canvas in layers? The same can be done with "Multi-Layered" letters.
Well, what effect does that have on me, Tony?

Quite a bit. There are, again, amazing things that can be done with each of these features. This tool wasn't put here by accident.

When you Ungroup a font to Layers, you're breaking it down to its barebones pieces, and you can leave it barebones or rebuild it however you want. You can also manipulate each layer, changing its color to fit better with your project.

You can also take the same layers and change the colors of them before Grouping them back together. You do this the same way you change the colors of the layers in your images. Choose "Print" in the "File" drop-down box. Then click the little colored-in box at the end of that field. You'll see a drop-box under that word, "Print Type," that says "Color" with many colors under it to choose from. You also have the option of clicking on that drop-box and changing "Color" to "Pattern." Doing that will give you an array of patterns to choose from. I chose a pattern for "Music" in the example below.

CURVING YOUR TEXT

Another fun tool in Cricut Design Space is "Curve." You'll find "Curve" between "Alignment" and "Advanced." When you click on "Curve," it throws down a slide bar for you. You slide the bar to the right to curve the words' ends down and left to curve them up.

In the screenshot below, you can see the straight line of text I started with. I Duplicated it, moved it up, and curved it to where it is now. The notes

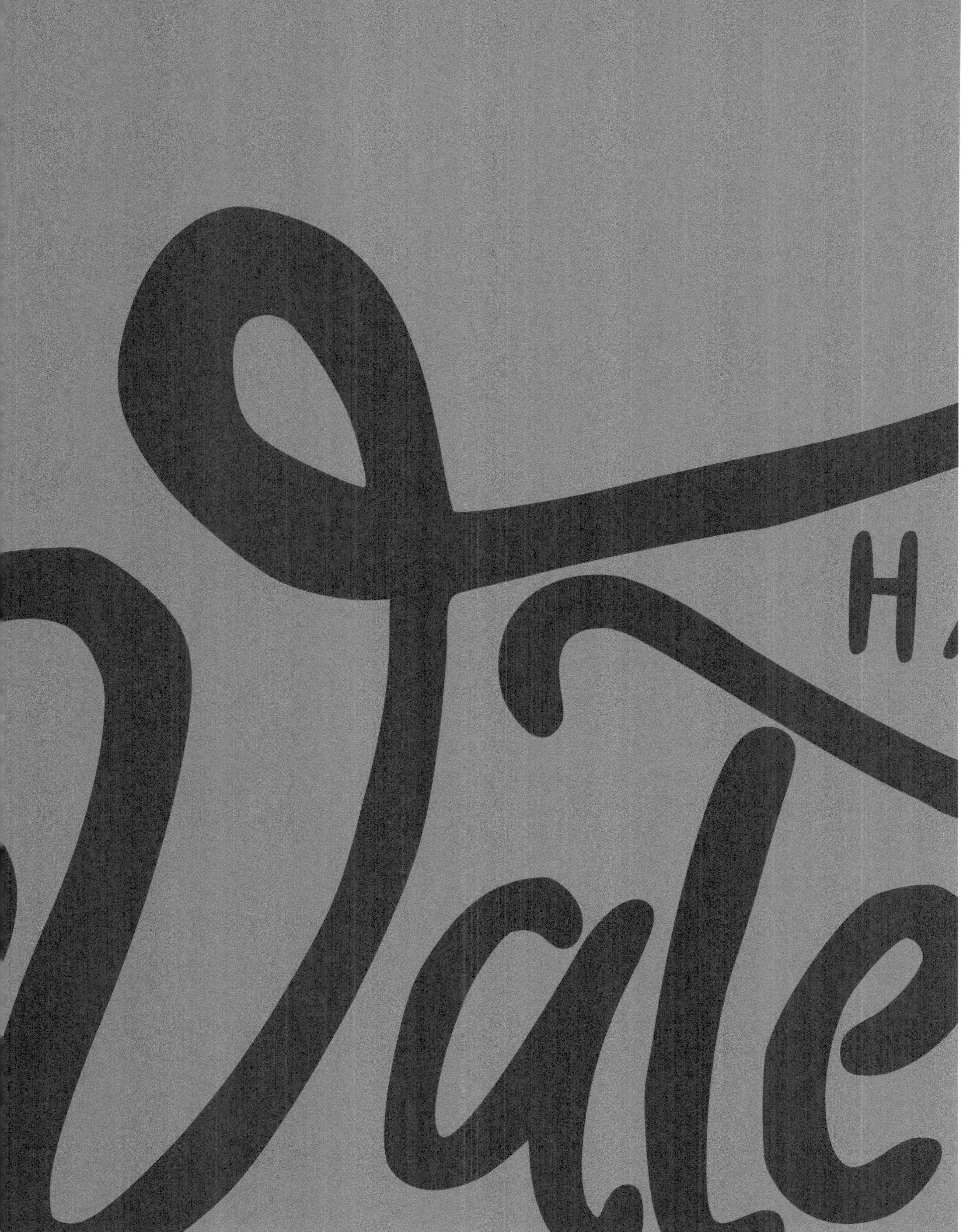

are images I inserted by clicking "Image" on the Design Panel.

If you thought curving that little bit of text was fun, you don't have to stop there. You can curve, un-curve, and recurve as many times as you want! Make sure you group your words so that they don't move on you after you have them exactly how you want them! I group several times at several stages just to be safe.

ATTACHING TEXT

You know how to attach images. Attaching text is precisely the same. The only difference is that you're going to take a few more steps to get there. Now you could just put the word there and attach it. Presto! Done! But, what's the fun in that? Instead, try Ungrouping your letters and placing them exactly where and how you want them. Then attach them! Another thing you want to remember: If you plan for your words to stay just like that to be cut out or printed instead of being thrown on their mats and cut out individually, be sure to Attach them or Weld them together!

MAKING A SHADOW

Another thing I do a lot with my machine is made shadows. It's effortless to do. There are two different ways I'm going to show you. The easy way and the hard way. I'll show you the hard way first since the easy way is my little shortcut.

FGHIJKL

TUVWXY

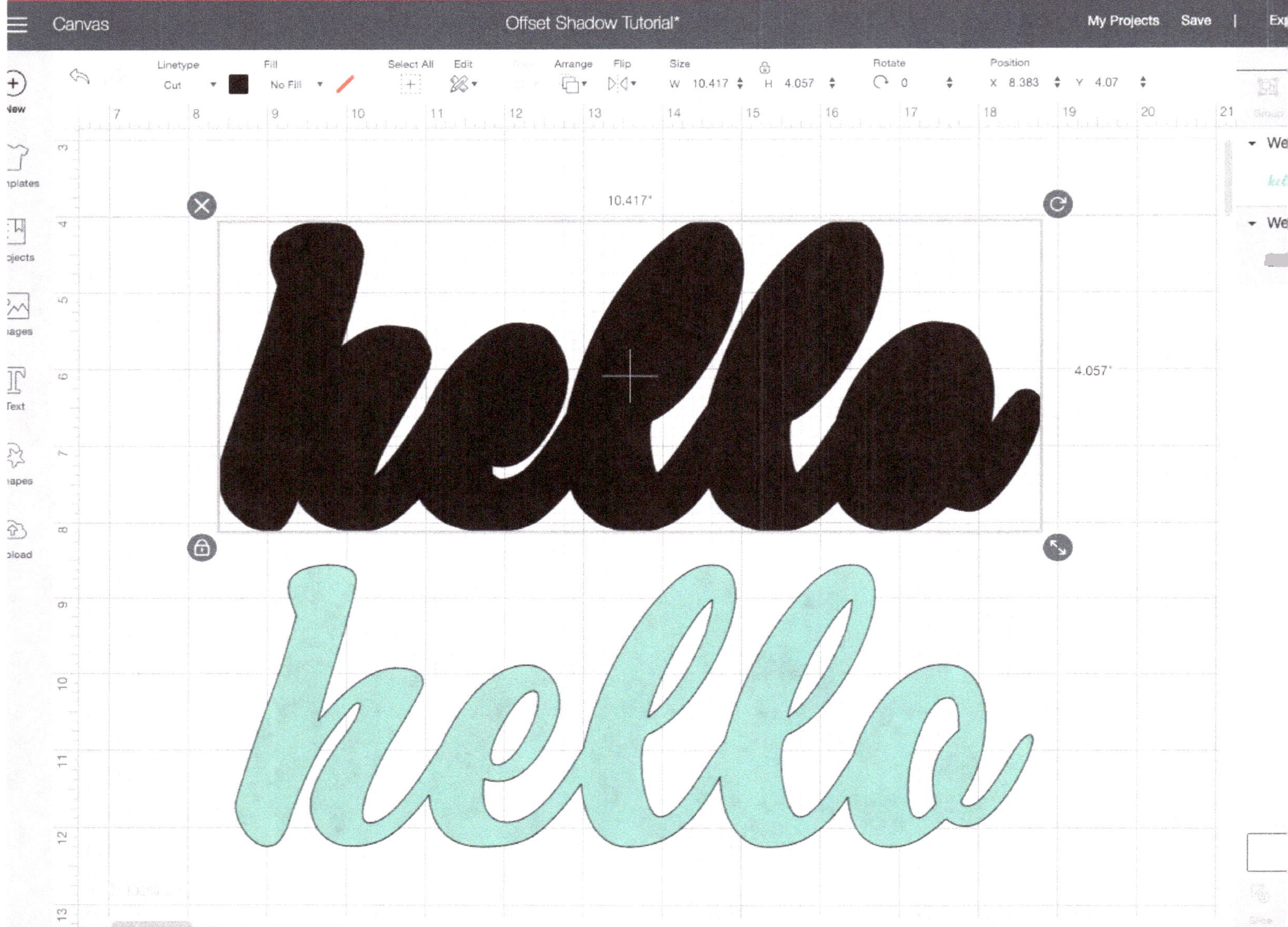
Linetype
Cut
Fill
No Fill
Select All
Edit
Arrange
Flip
Size
W 10.417
H 4.057
Rotate
0
Position
X 8.383
Y 4.07
10.417"
4.057"
hello
hello

·Both ways start the same:

·Click "Text" and type in what you'd like. I'm using my name.

·Choose your font.

·Make it bold.

·Move the letters as close together as you want them. Remember that you can "Ungroup to Letters" to get them lined up just perfectly if you want to.
·Weld them together.

·Drag your text until it's as close to 9 inches across the top as you can get it.

·Change the "Fill" drop-down box on the Text Edit Bar from "No Fill" to "Print."

·Click "Make It" in the top right-hand corner.

·After you click on "Make It," you're going to click on "Continue."

·When you do, it will bring up this next box:

·Click the toggle to turn "Use System Dialog" on.

·Click "Print." This screen will pop up:

·In the bottom left-hand corner, you'll see a drop-down box that says, "PDF." Click that and tell your computer to "Open in Preview."

·In the Preview screen, click "File" and "Save." When it asks you to name the file, change the PDF format to PNG by clicking on the drop-box by "Format."

·Save the file to your desktop for easy finding.

·Closeout of the program you're previewing your file on.

·Go back to Cricut Design Space. Cancel the print and the cut.

·Click "Upload File" on the Design Panel.

·Click "Simple Image" since that's what you're uplo-ading.

·The next screen will give you the chance to erase all the yuck and do some cleanup. Click everything you want going. That would be the background, the line around your word, and the holes inside and in-between the letters.

·Click "Insert."

·Select "Save As Cut Image."

·Once your word is on your Canvas, you'll have to rotate it. Place the word on top of it that it originally came from.

·Make sure you have your "Original Word" the color you want it.

·Group the two layers. Voila!

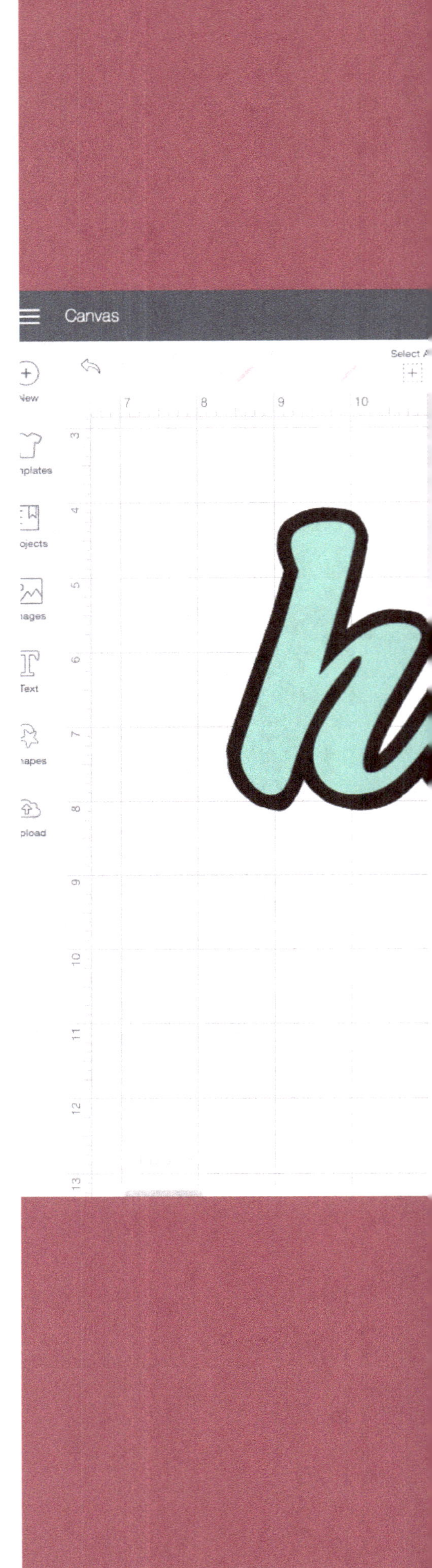

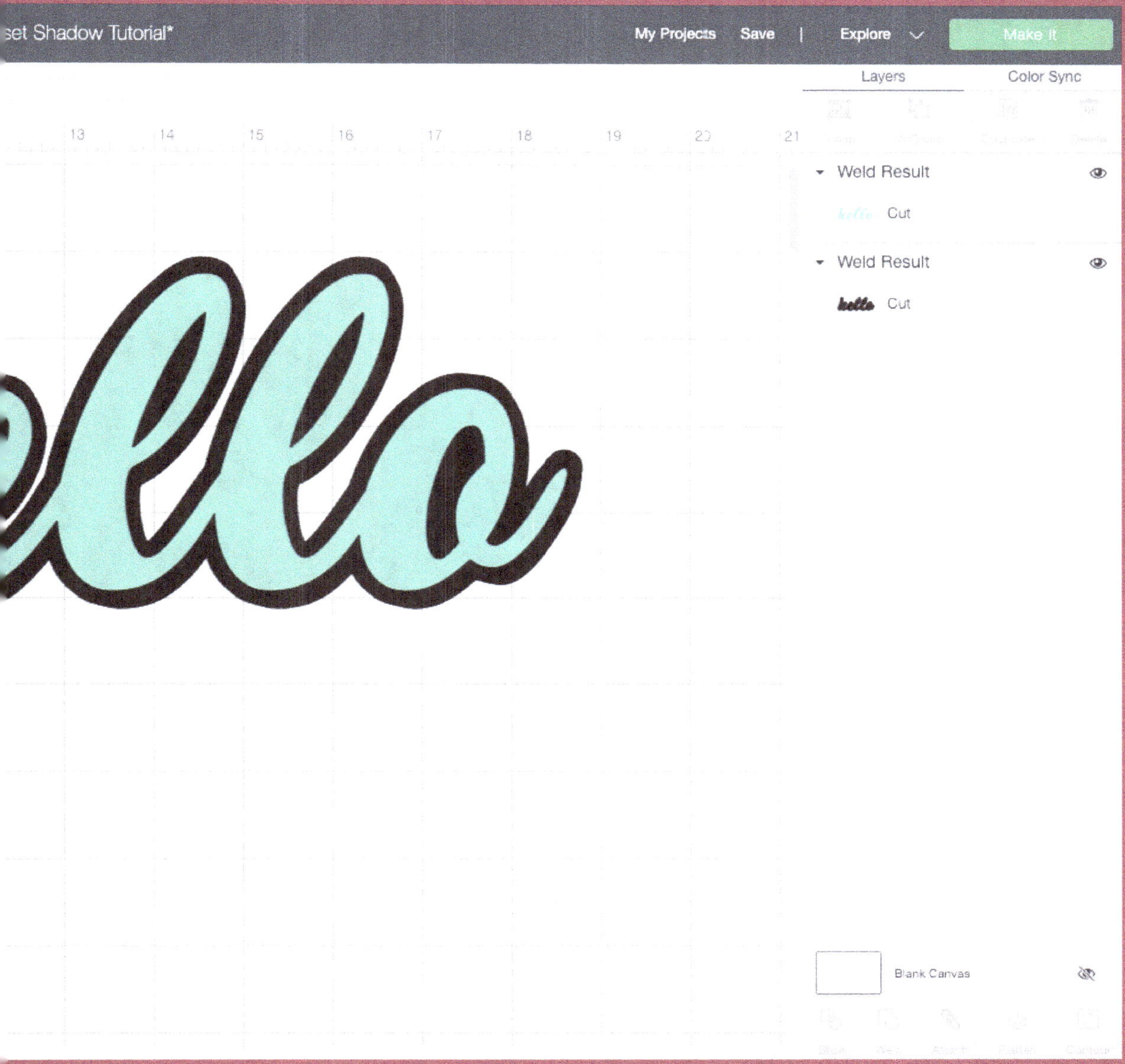

set Shadow Tutorial*
My Projects   Save | Explore ⌄   Make It
Layers   Color Sync
▾ Weld Result   ◉
   hello Cut
▾ Weld Result   ◉
   hello Cut
13   14   15   16   17   18   19   20   21
Blank Canvas   ⦸

How to Use Images

Selecting the image you want to use can be fun. There are so many to choose from, and you'll enjoy browsing the library.

You'll want to start by browsing the Cricut Image Library. There you will find cartridges, called image sets, where you can choose your designs.

HOW TO BROWSE AND SEARCH FOR CARTRIDGES

First, select the "images" icon in the design panel to the left of the canvas. A new window should appear with the Image Library. You'll next select the "cartridges" tab at the top of the screen to browse all the available cartridges. There are over 400 cartridges to choose from. You should see the cartridge name and a sample of the image. It will tell you if the cartridge is free or if it can be purchased individually or is a part of the subscription plan.

You don't have to search alphabetically. You can type all or part of a cartridge name into the search bar and click on the magnifying glass icon. You then click "view all images" to browse your search results.

Once you've made your selection, simply click the "Insert Images" button, and they will be added to the canvas. Once added to the canvas, you can size your image(s) and move them around on the can-

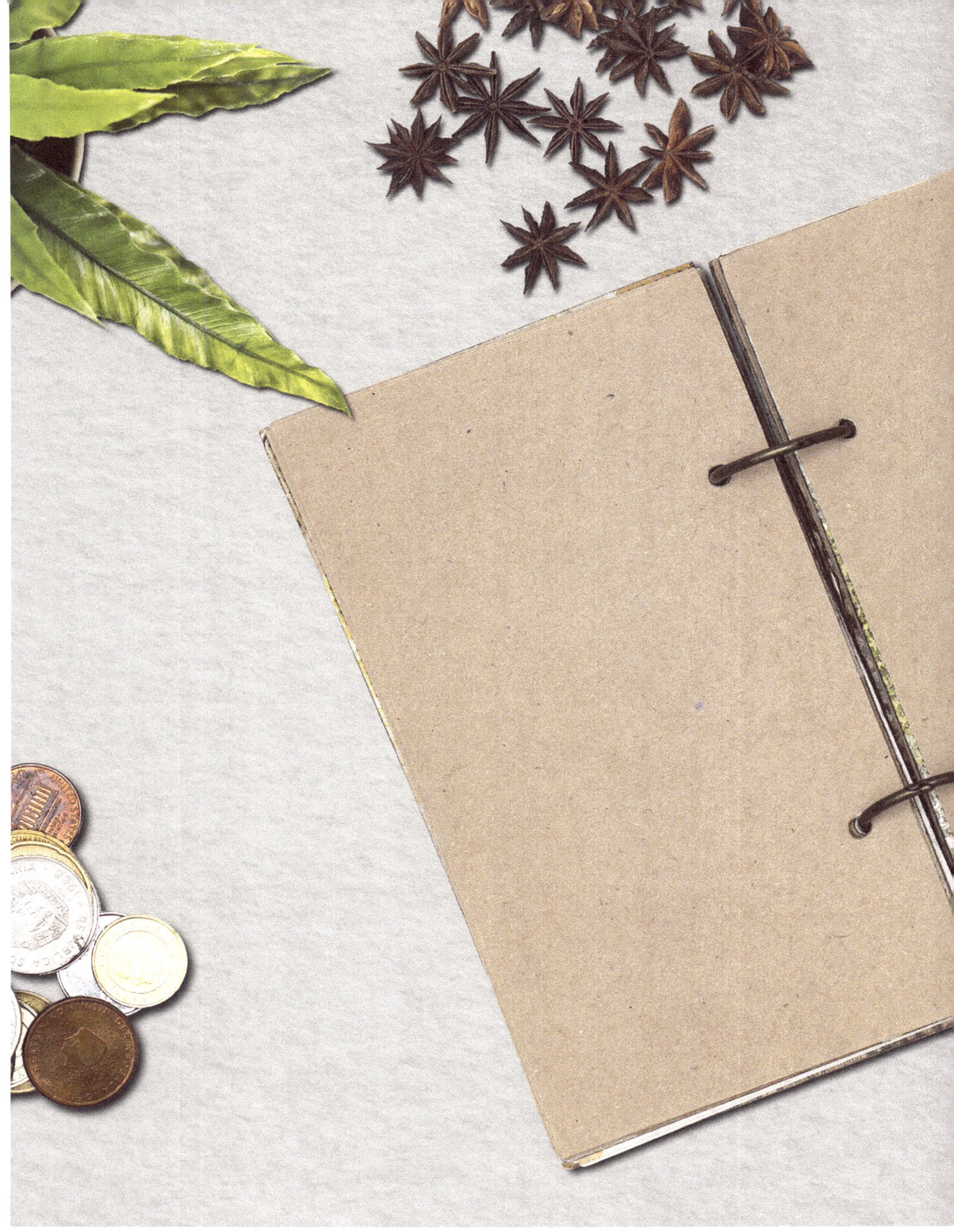

vas. You can get an idea of where you want your image and how it will look on your final project. It can be more cost-effective to purchase entire cartridges than purchase individual images if your selection isn't included in the free offerings.

SEARCHING FOR CARTRIDGE WITH FILTERS

If you want to search for cartridges with filters, you simply click on the cartridge icon and select the Filters menu in the top right corner of the screen. This will bring up all available filters.

There are three ways to search: alphabetical order, cartridge type, or by the specific cartridge. When you find the filter you want, select "Apply" to transfer it to your canvas.

HOW TO PURCHASE IMAGES

• My Cartridges include all free cartridges, linked, purchased, and part of Cricut Access. You must be a member to have access to these.

• Free - These cartridges can be used without a subscription or a one-time purchase.

• Cricut Access - These cartridges are accessible with your subscription.

• Purchased - These are the cartridges you've already purchased and are added to your canvas. These are your four options for obtaining images. I've included how to access them for free for those who don't want to spend money on images or have their own.

It's good to check the Cricut website for any price changes and the features each subscription entitles you to.

UPLOADING YOUR IMAGES

You can upload your own images in the file formats .png, .gif, .jpg, .bmp, .dxf, and .svg,
Design Space will let you upload your images for
free and will convert them into shapes that you
can cut.
There are two different ways your images are
uploaded, depending on the file type.
Basic images are compatible with .gif, .jpg,.png, and
.bmp file types. When uploaded, these files can be
a single layer, and you can edit the images throughout the upload course.
Vector images include .svg and .dxf file types.
These files are designed before you upload them
to your canvas. They will routinely be disconnected
into layers afterward uploading then saving.
To begin a basic upload, click Upload from the
Design Panel on the screen's left side. A window
will open and prompt you to choose an image or
pattern to upload. Click the image you want and
click the upload icon again. It's that simple!

HOW TO EDIT IMAGES USING THE SLICE TOOL

Many Cricut users do all their editing separately because it seems too difficult to do on the machine.
Let's walk through the process, so you'll be able to
do this with ease once you've had a little practice.
First, you need to include your uploaded photos to
your canvas by clicking on the image then select
"Insert Images." You can add one more image at

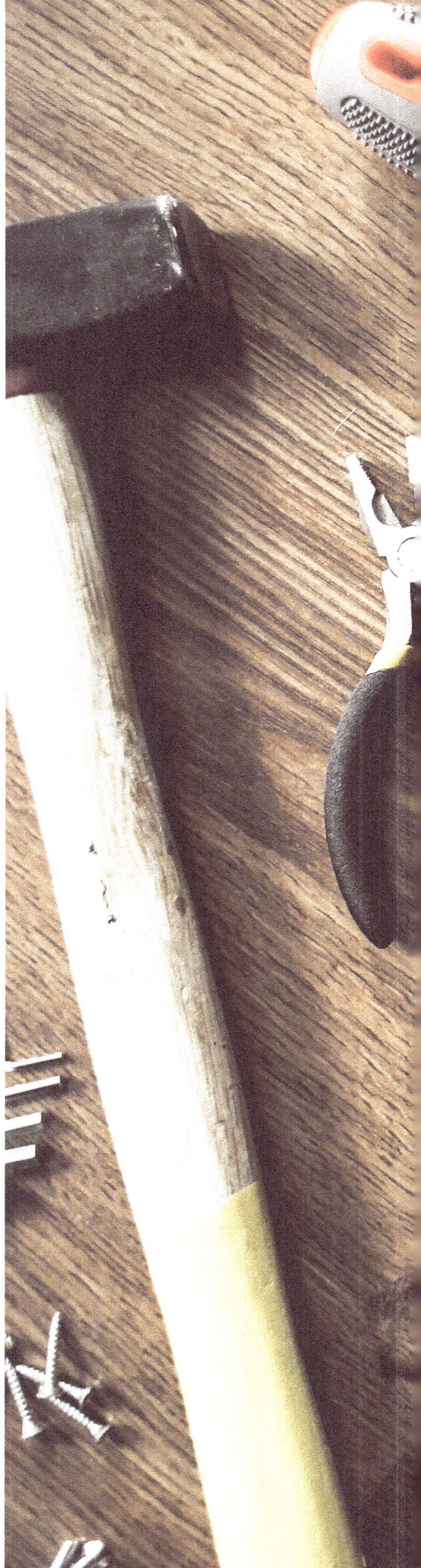

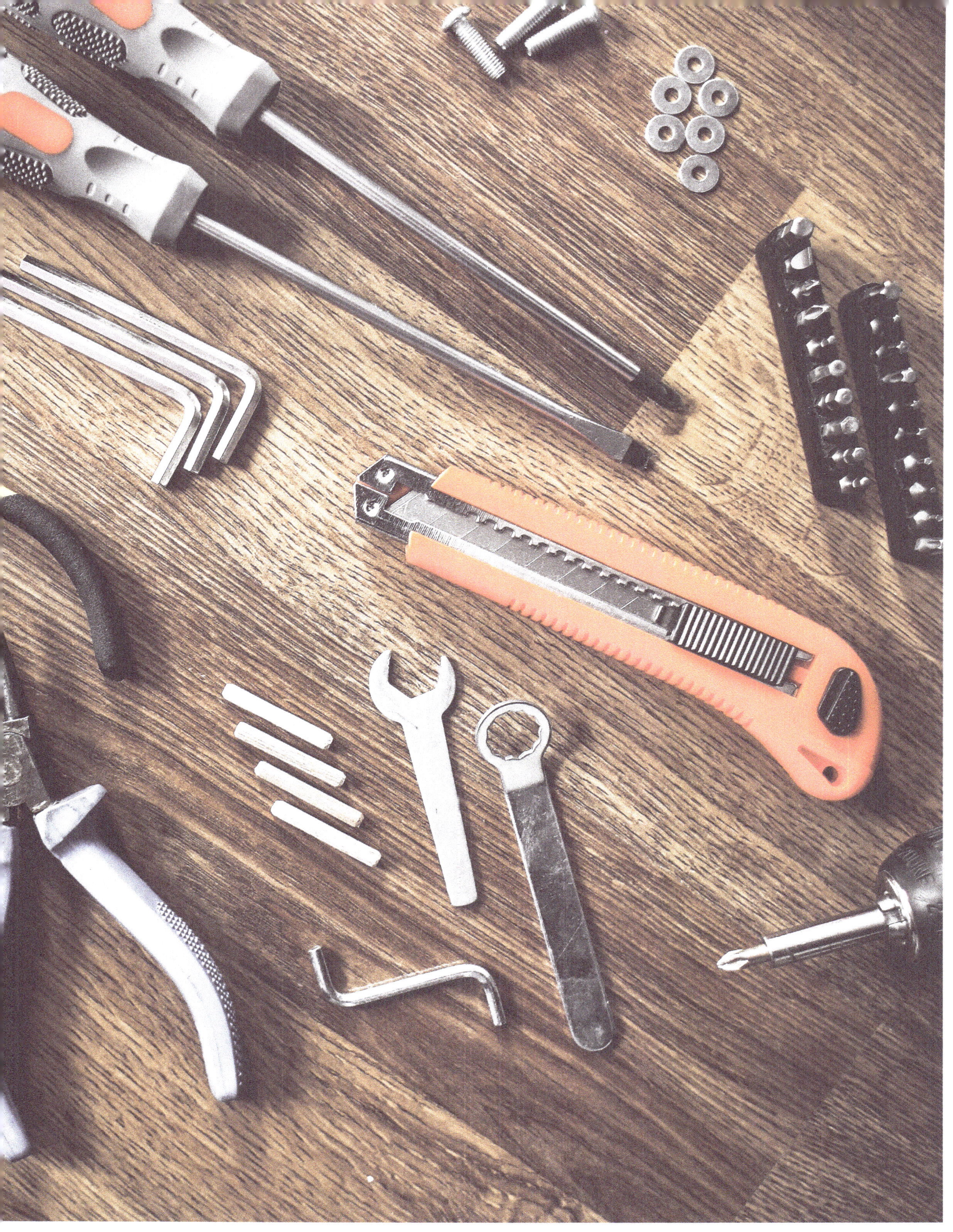

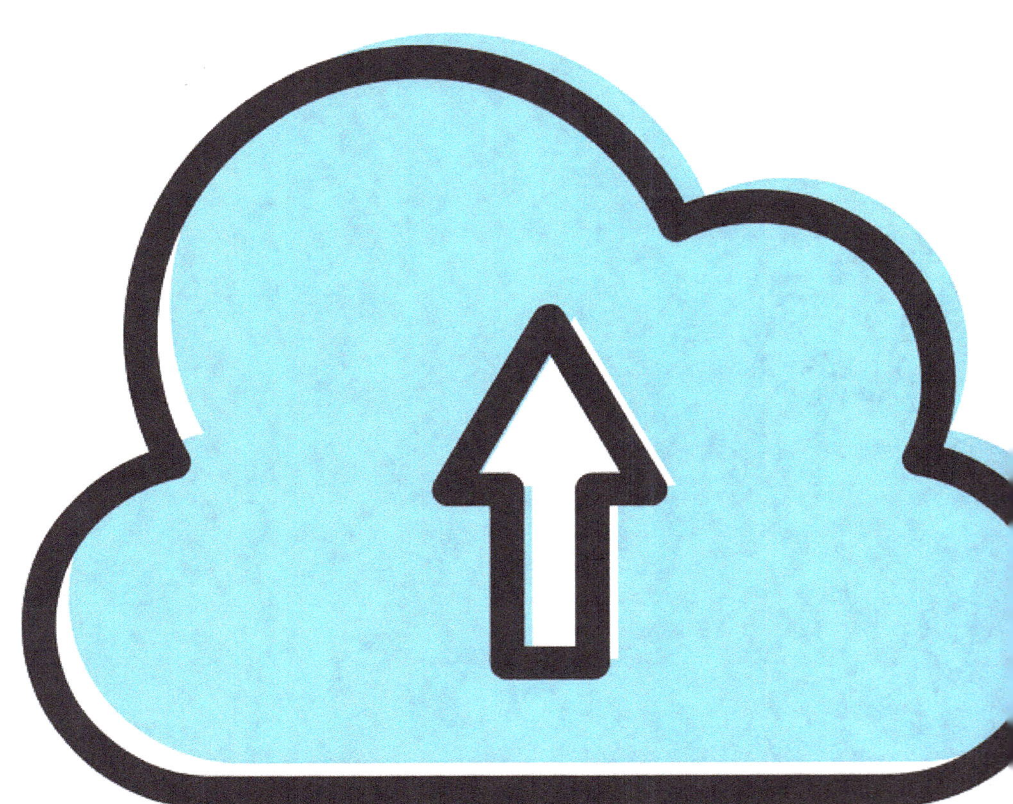

this time.

You can make your image a bit bigger if you need to. Click the right-bottom corner and drag it down so you can see it better.

There's no erase option, so if something in your image you don't want, you'll have to use the Slice tool. This can be a bit more difficult than merely erasing with the eraser tool.

You'll need to click on "Shapes" on the left side and click the square. You'll see a lock icon on the left-bottom of the circle just below the square. This will unlock it and give you the freedom to move it wherever you'd like.

Place it over the part of the image you want to erase. This should bring up a bubble. Your square and your image should be highlighted. Make sure they are and click the Slice tool. You'll find it in the bottom-right corner.

You can begin to pull away from the pieces and delete them. You may have to repeat this several times before you've erased the parts of the image that you want going. This will depend on the size of your erasure.

Be sure to save your changes.

EDITING IMAGES IN UPLOAD MODE

This is an easy process for editing your uploaded image. But first, you need to upload an image from your computer.

When it's uploaded, click on the complete icon, and a window should open. Look to the top-left corner of your canvas, and you should see a wand. Place it over the part of the image you want to erase and click once. Click continue, and you'll need to type in a name for your image and click the save button. That part of the image should be gone. You'll repeat the steps for each part of the image you want to be erased.

When you have erased everything you want, you need to make sure it's named before saving it and closing it.

Add both photos to your Cricut Design Space canvas. When you have them there, you can put them back together.

The nice thing about this feature is that you can do more than erase. If you want to change color, the same process applies.

Editing doesn't have to be a difficult task, and the more you get to know your Circuit and the Design Space, the easier it will be to upload and edit your images.

CREATE LAYERS AND SEPARATE OBJECTS

There are many features for creating layers. This can be complex if you're not accustomed to using the many features your Cricut offers. We will review them separately so you can understand each one. You will want to practice before cutting your project.

· Group/Ungroup - You can group multiple layers, images, or text using the group function. They will move and size together on your design canvas.

· The ungroup function will let you move and size layers, images, or text separately.

· Duplicate - To duplicate an object, you simply copy and paste to create the same object's multiples.

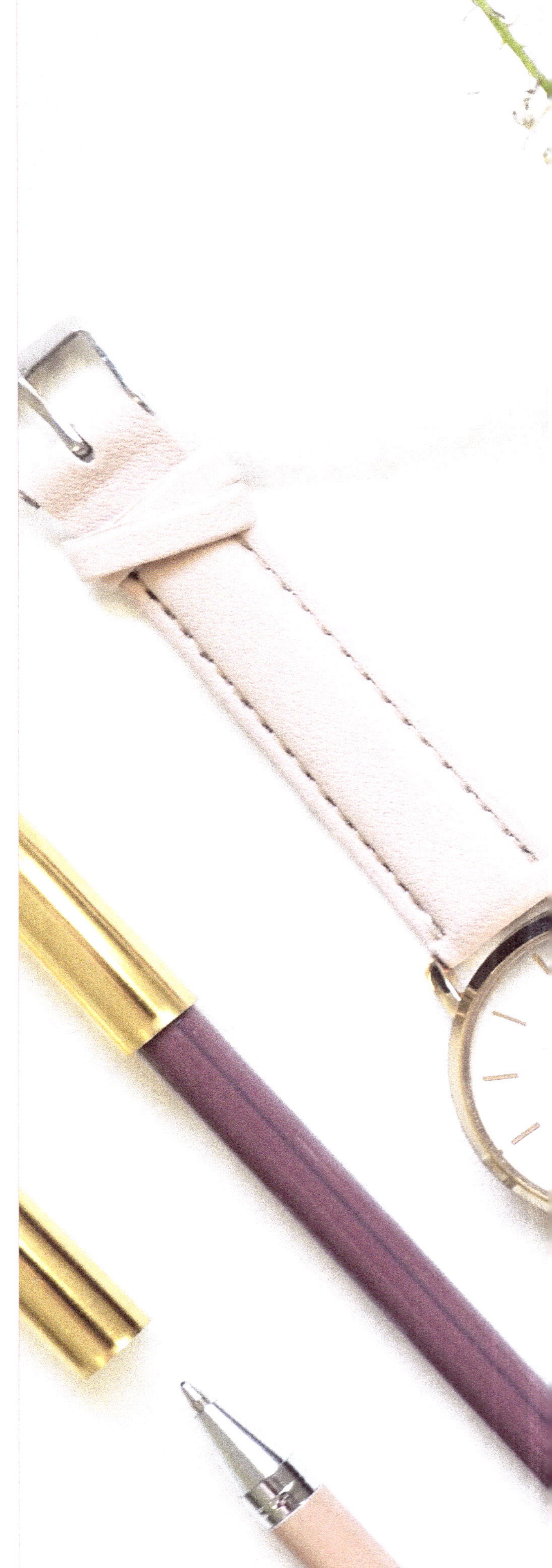

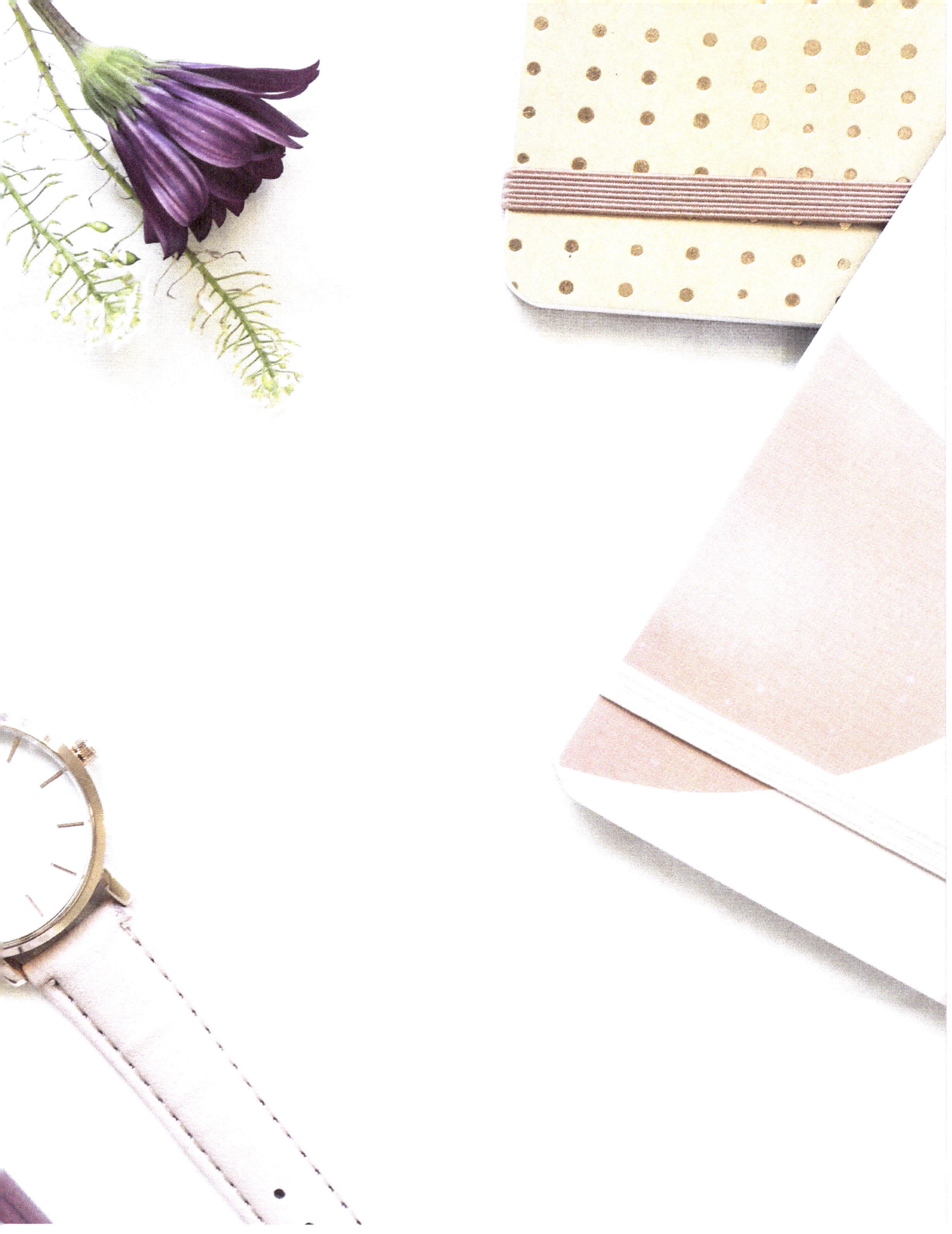

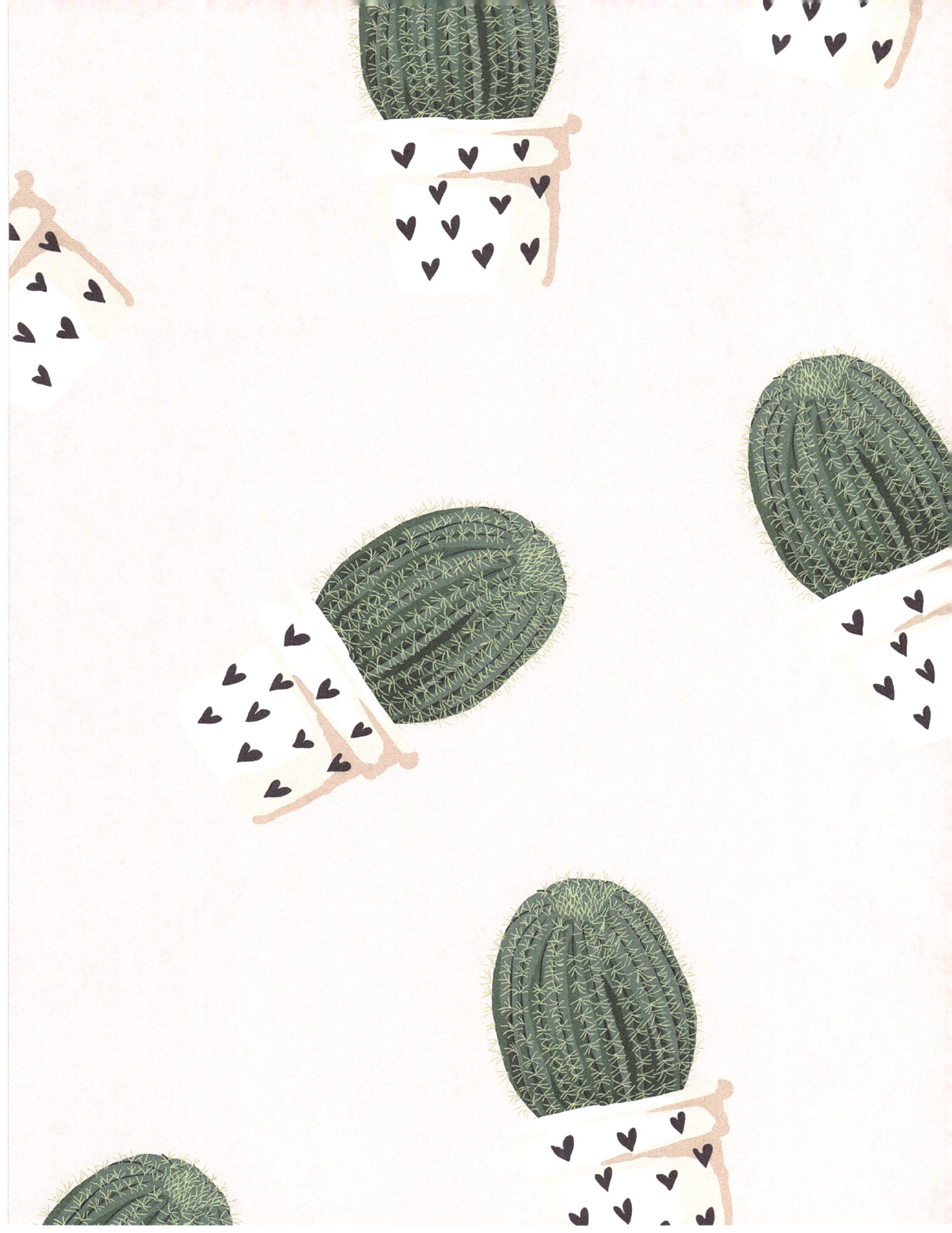

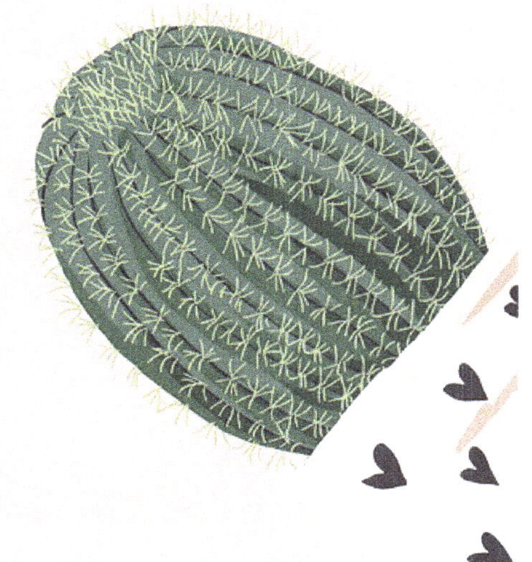

·   Delete - Deleting will remove your selected object from the canvas. If you do this in error, you can undo this action.

·   Slice - Slicing will split two overlapping layers.

·   Weld - When you want to join multiple layers to create one object, use the meld function.

·   Attach/Detach - When you attach, you hold your objects in position so that objects will cut, draw, or score separately from the other layers.

·   Flatten/Unflatten - When you want to convert an image into a printable image, use the fatter feature. This will merge the layers you selected into a single layer. Unflatten does the opposite, separating layers from one printable image into separate printable layers.

·   Contour - Contouring will cut paths on a layer or hide or show contour lines. If your image uses more than one layer, be sure to Ungroup first for Contour to work.

·   Visible/Hidden Layer - When the eyeball icon s open, it points to that the layer is evident on the canvas, and it's safe to cut, draw score or print. Hidden layers will not draw, cut, score, or print, and you simply click the icon to hide them. Click again to unhide.

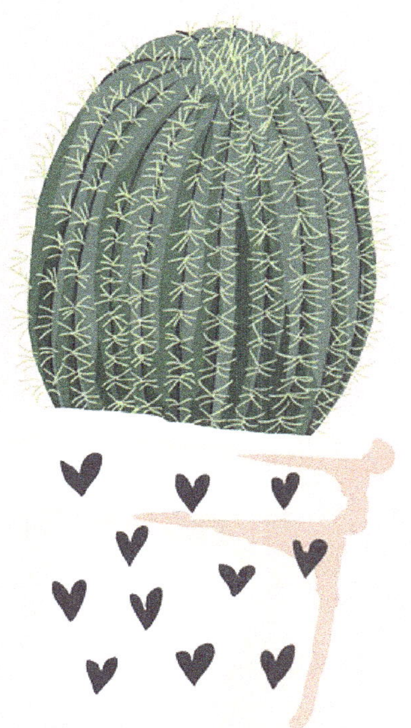

Chapter 4
Cricut Design Space Tips and Tricks

REGISTER TO CRICUT ACCESSIBILITY

If you want to get the utmost from owning a Cricut Research Air two, we then advocate subscribing to Cricut Accessibility. It is possible to pay a monthly fee of about $10, or maybe a yearly fee that proves to be marginally cheaper per month.

Cricut access provides you access to 30,000+ images, 1000's jobs, and quite 370 fonts; if you are likely to use your Cricut a whole lot, then that will save an excellent deal of money than if you ought to get every undertaking and picture separately.

Plus, it's less of a hassle to hide a group rate than stressing about just how much cash you are spending on projects! It adds up! Make your money's worth from your Cricut by creating fantastic Design Space jobs.

DE-TACK YOUR CUTTING MAT

De-tack your Cricut cutting mat a bit!
The Explore Air 2 typically includes the green ordinary cutting mat, although the Maker generally will accompany the whole grim light clasp mat.

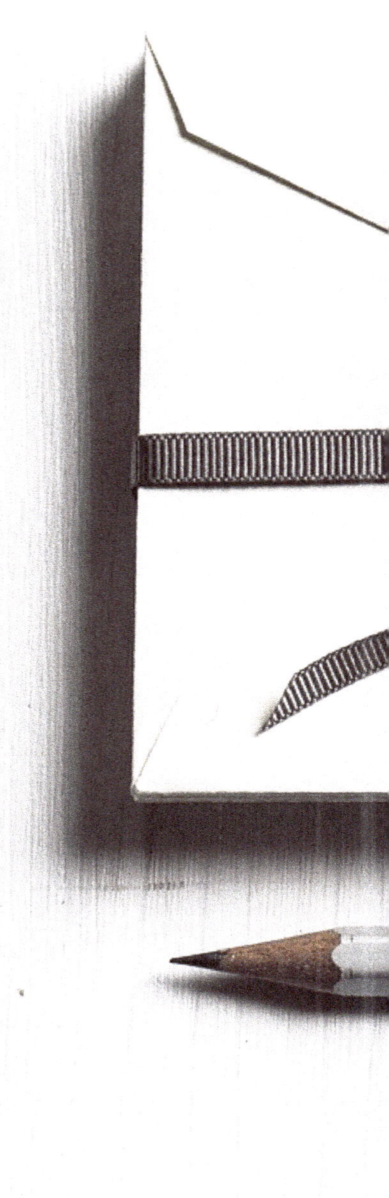

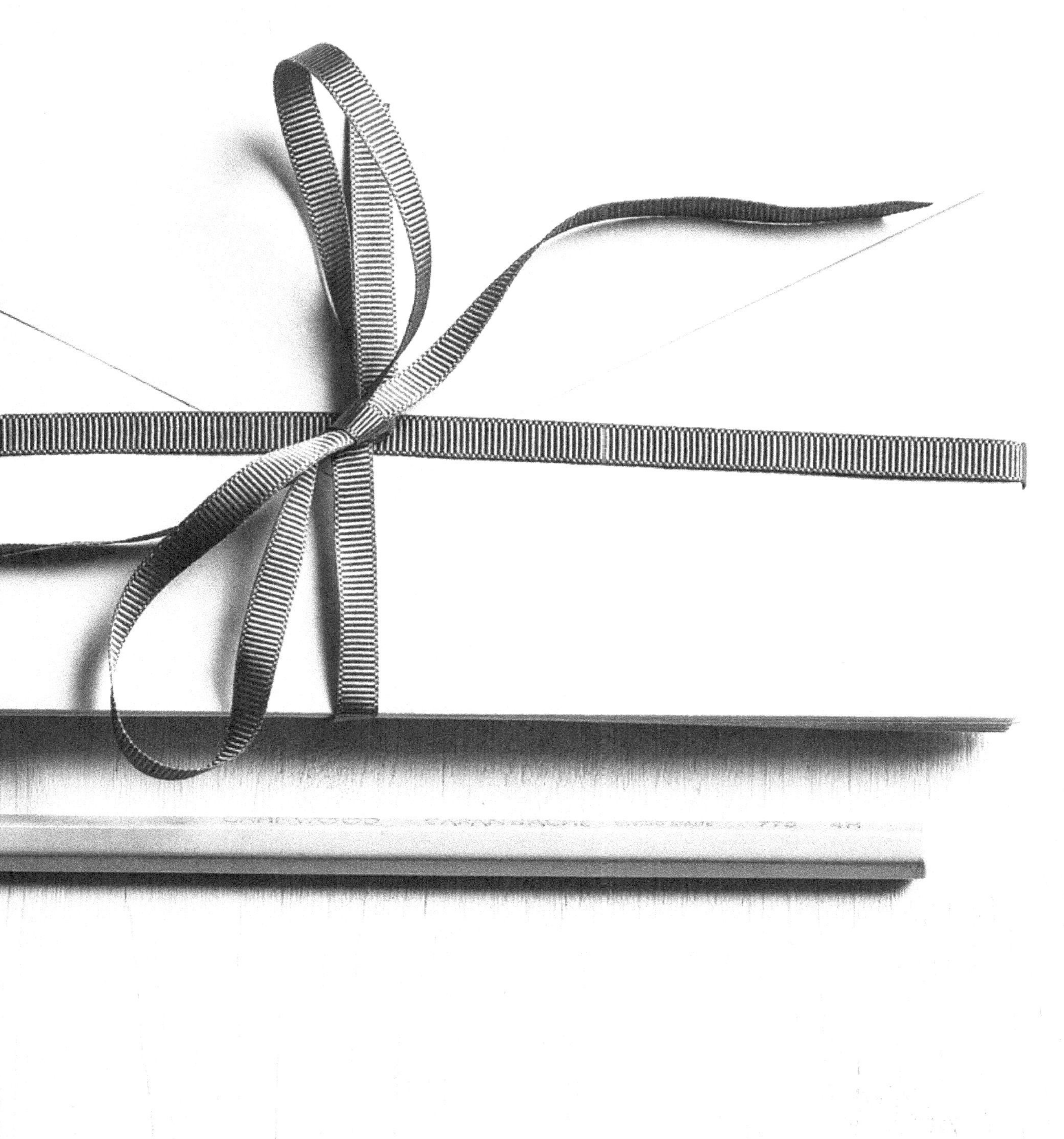

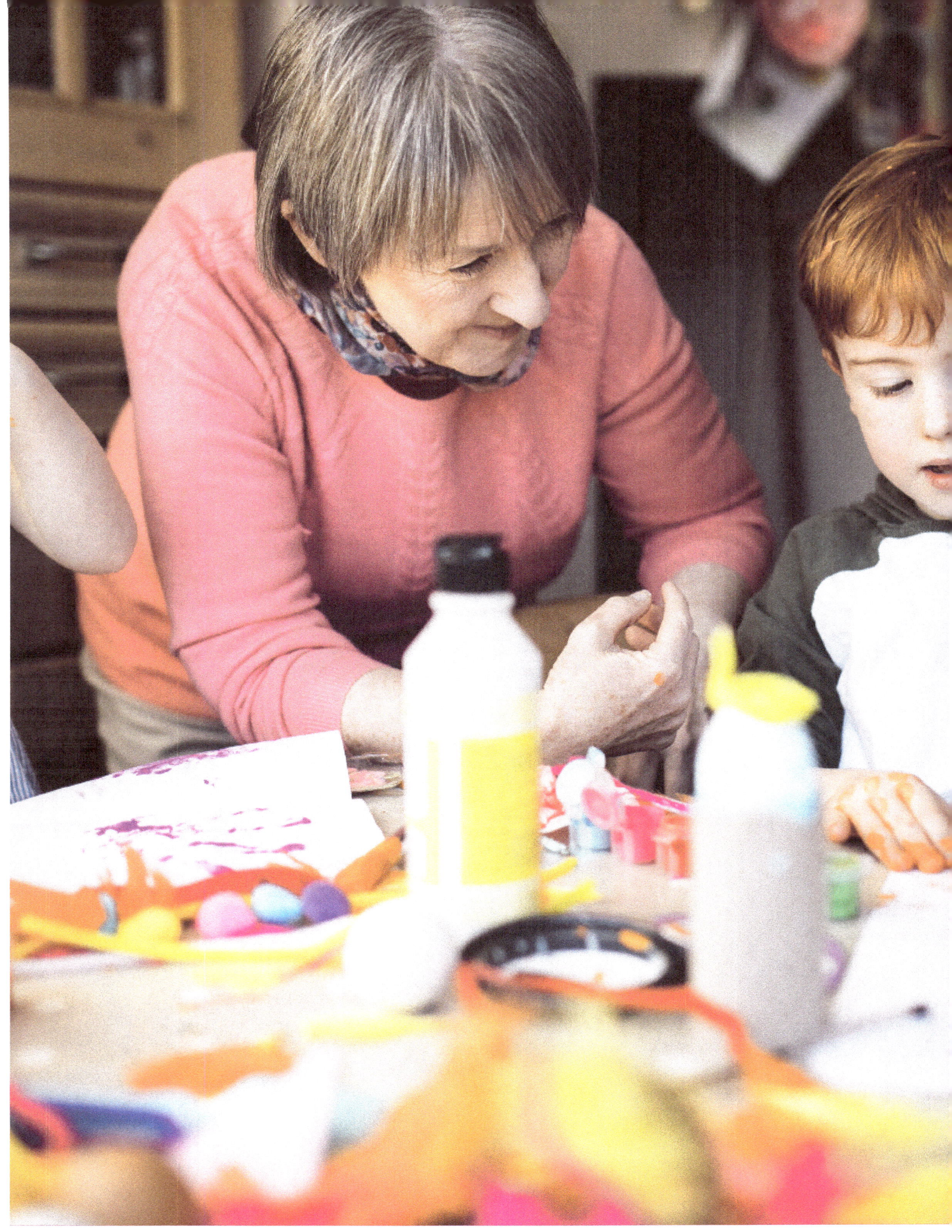

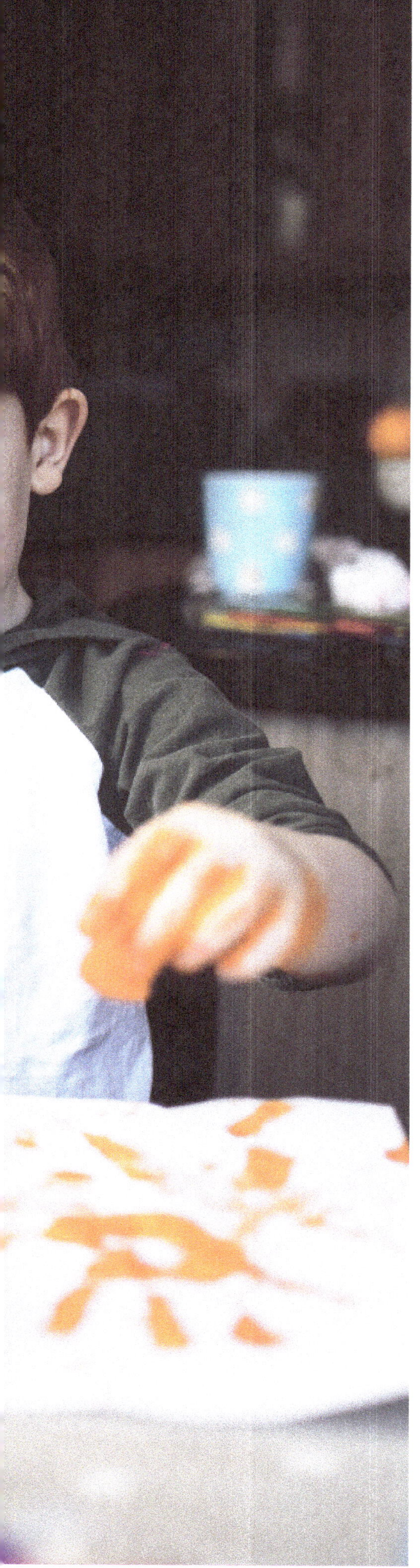

You set your stuff on the mat before placing it in the machine.

The green cutting mat is somewhat tacky when new! Once you peel off the plastic get through, you will put a clean, sterile t-shirt in the mat to prime it to your very first job. It is quite tough to accumulate the cardstock off, even if you have all of the resources when it is in its real stickiness! It is simple to harm the project while attempting to get off it.

You should not have this issue with the grim light clasp mat, which suggests you would possibly also buy that for your card and paper jobs instead of de-tacking the mat.

MAINTAIN YOUR CUTTING MAT COVERS

The cutting mats include a Plastic shield. This might be pulled away and placed back quickly. We maintained our pay and put back our mat once we are through with this; it retains the mat tacky and clean longer!

FIXING THE CRICUT CUTTING MAT

Every once in a while (or even whenever you use it), provide your cutting mat a wash-over with a couple of baby wipes.

The non-alcohol water packs without aroma are best. This will help keep it freed from using cardstock and plastic residue out of the leading edge and the average family dust and lint drifting around.

Get the Perfect Tools

It includes a useful instrument, also a scraper, tweezers, and a spatula alongside scissors. It's particularly beneficial to possess the weeding tool if you consider cutting adhesive plastic or heat transport vinyl.

THE CRICUT SCORING STYLUS

So, varieties of cardboard jobs require that you get the scoring stylus. I didn't purchase one with my equipment initially and thus needed to wait for it to arrive until I actually could do a far better job. If you bought your system as a part of a package, it'd possess the scoring stylus contained, so countercheck.

START WITH THE SAMPLE PROJECT

Once your device arrives, begin with the sample job.

The research air two and maker include sample stuff for an initial job. Unless you buy a Cricut Bundle, you get the minimum number of stuff to do this small thing. However, it is ideal to start simple!

Instead of attempting to do anything big and elaborate, start here to find out how things work, software and hardware-wise.

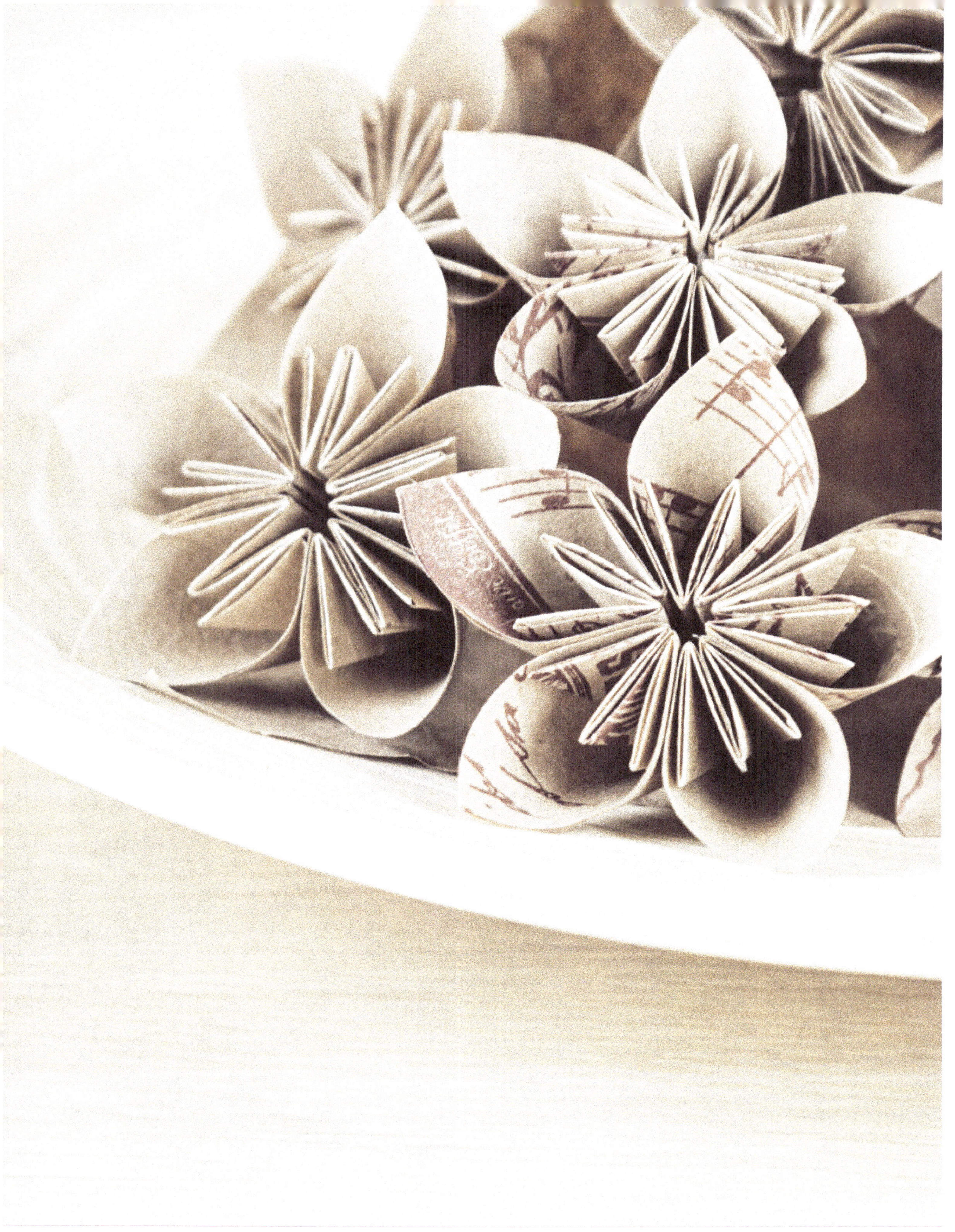

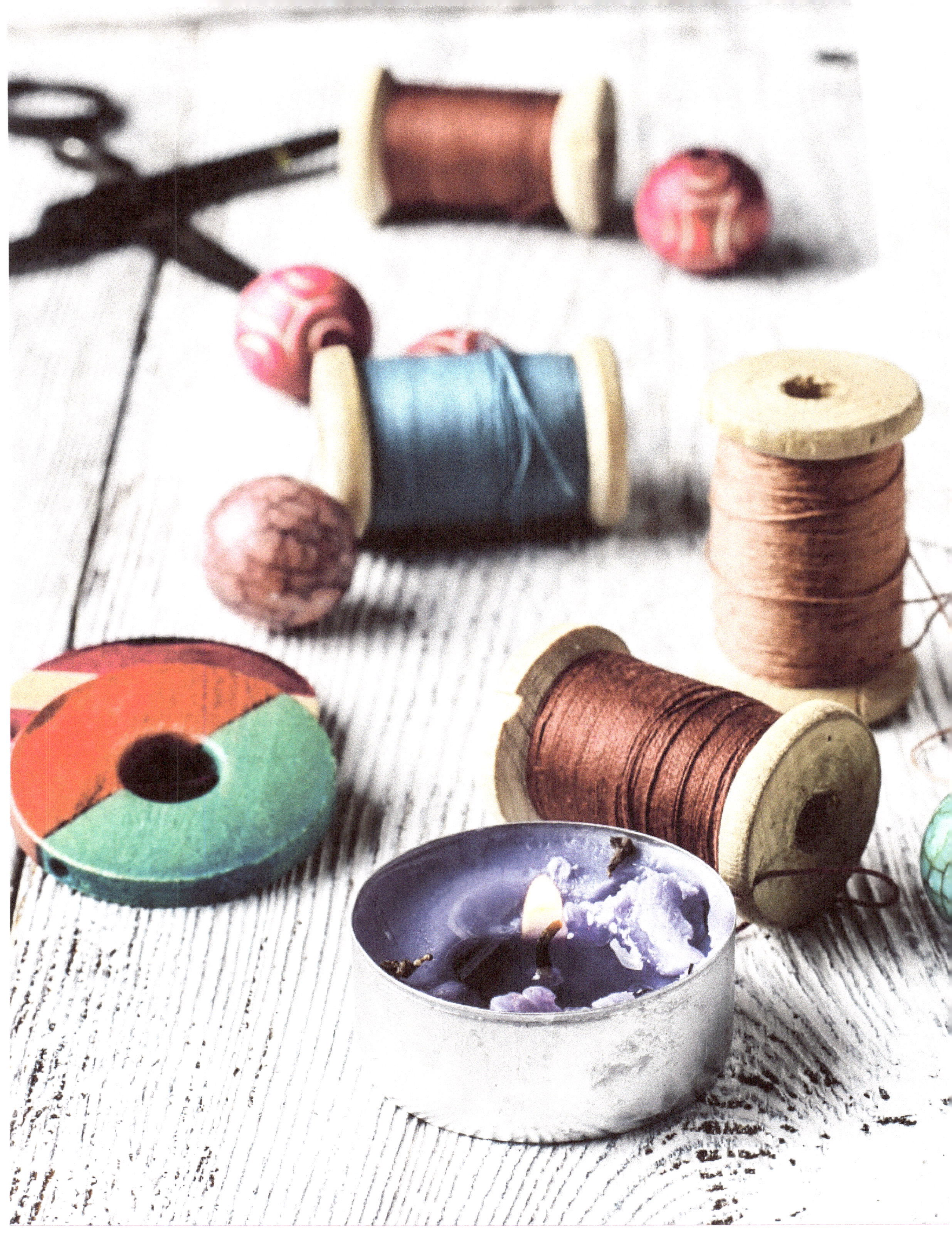

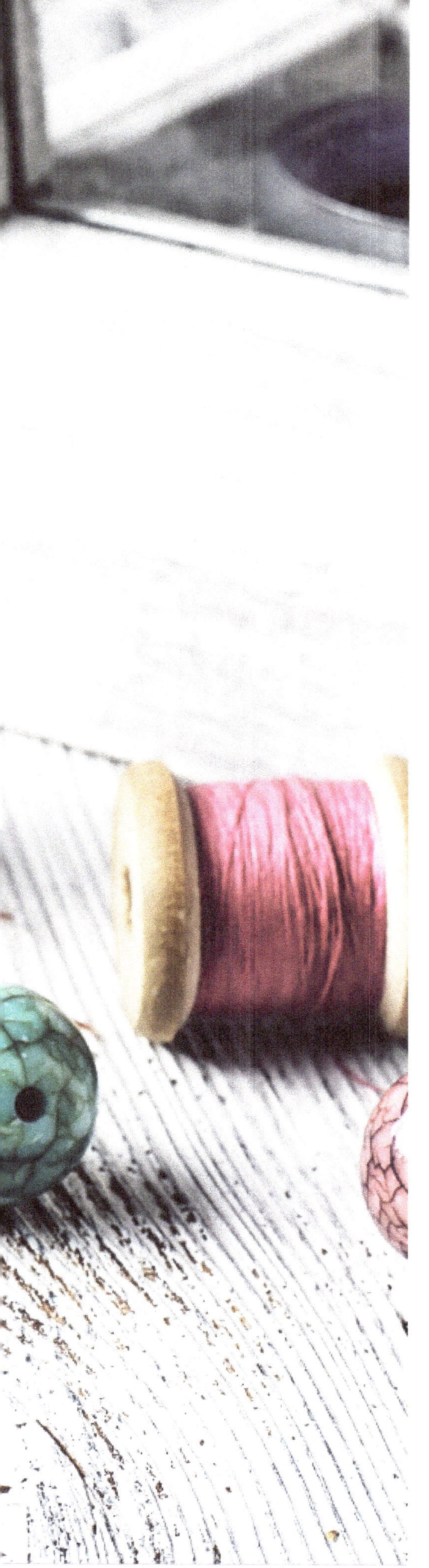

EVALUATION CUTS

After doing all of your jobs, it will be sensible to perform a test cut before doing the whole thing. If the blade has been set too low, it will destroy your cutting mat. When it is overlarge, it'd just cut marginally through your cardstock, vinyl, etc., and destruct your supplies.

Having a test trimming may include requesting your system to cut a little circle.

Check the atmosphere is correct and make adjustments if needed.

ALTER PEN LIDS AFTER UTILIZATION

It is vita to possess the lid on it A.s.a.p. after you have finished using it, it will not dry out. They are too costy to waste. The neat thing about the design Space jobs is the indisputable fact that it frequently prompts you to set the lid back!

AGED CRICUT CARTRIDGES

Do not forget to attach any older Cartridges you would possibly have gotten from a former device to your account. This is often a relatively straightforward process, as displayed below.

Each chance can be connected after, so if you are looking at purchasing some second user, then affirm that this has not been achieved yet! Besides using the proper tools to eliminate your cardstock or plastic in the top mat, there is just another trick to getting off it.

Rather than peeling your project from the mat that would cause curling (or overall mangling), peel away the mat from the undertaking. Bend the mat from the cardboard rather than the other way round.

PURCHASE THE DEEP CUT BLADE

There is nothing worse than putting your heart into a project than finding you do not have the perfect tools!

The heavy cut blade lets one cut deeper leather, card, chipboard, and far more. This blade works with all the Explore Air 2. It is necessary not just to get the blade but the blade casing too.

FREE SVG DOCUMENTS

You do not need only to use layouts in the design space shop. You will either make your SVG documents or use other free SVG documents that can be found all around the World Wide Web.

LOAD MAT CORRECTLY

Ensure that your mat is correctly filled before you start cutting. It needs to slide beneath the rollers. Your device will probably just begin cutting before the grid's cap onto the mat or perhaps not if it is not loaded directly.

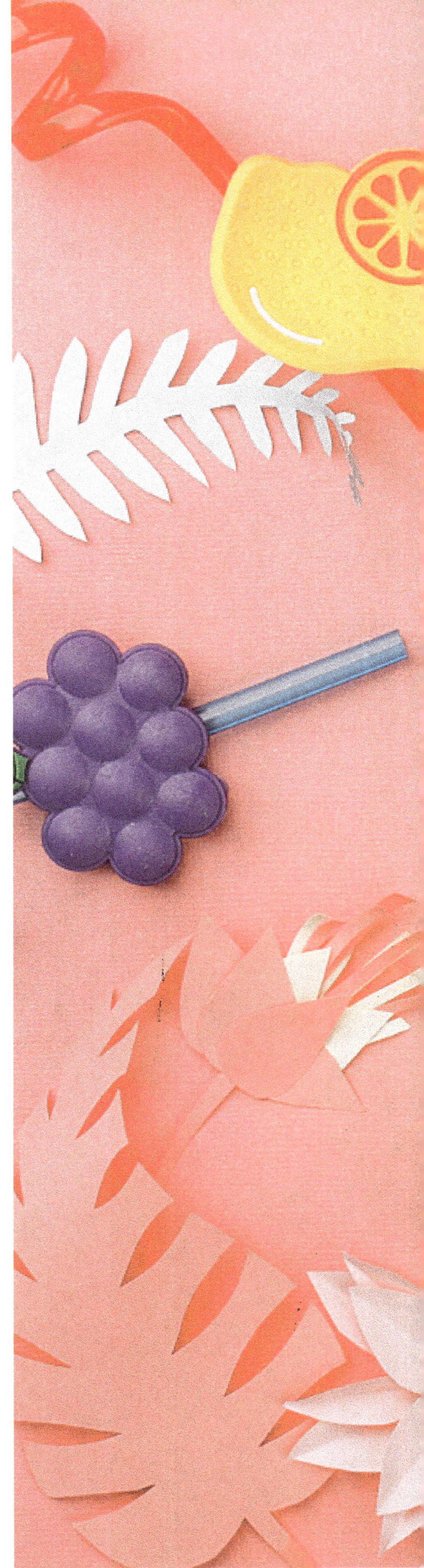

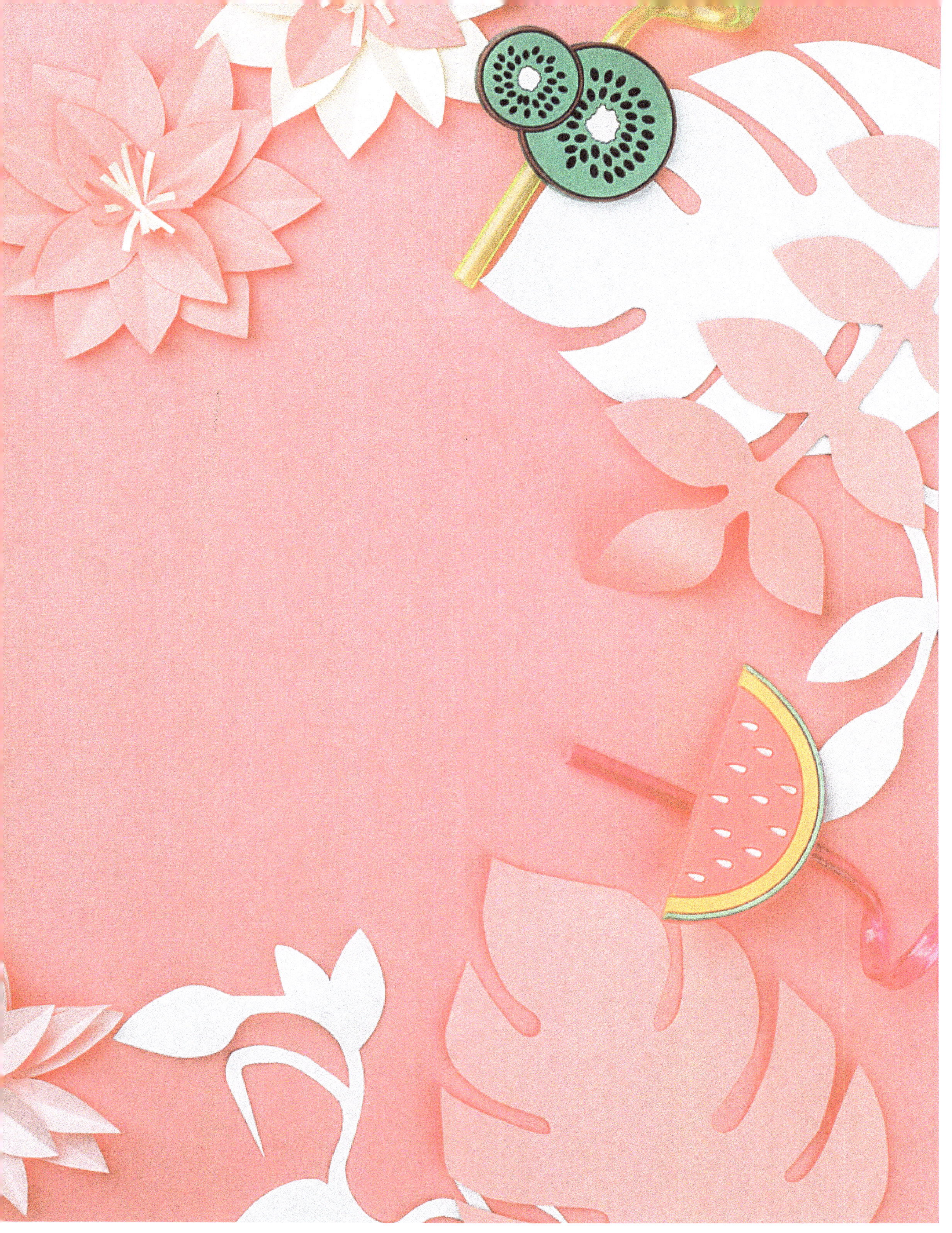

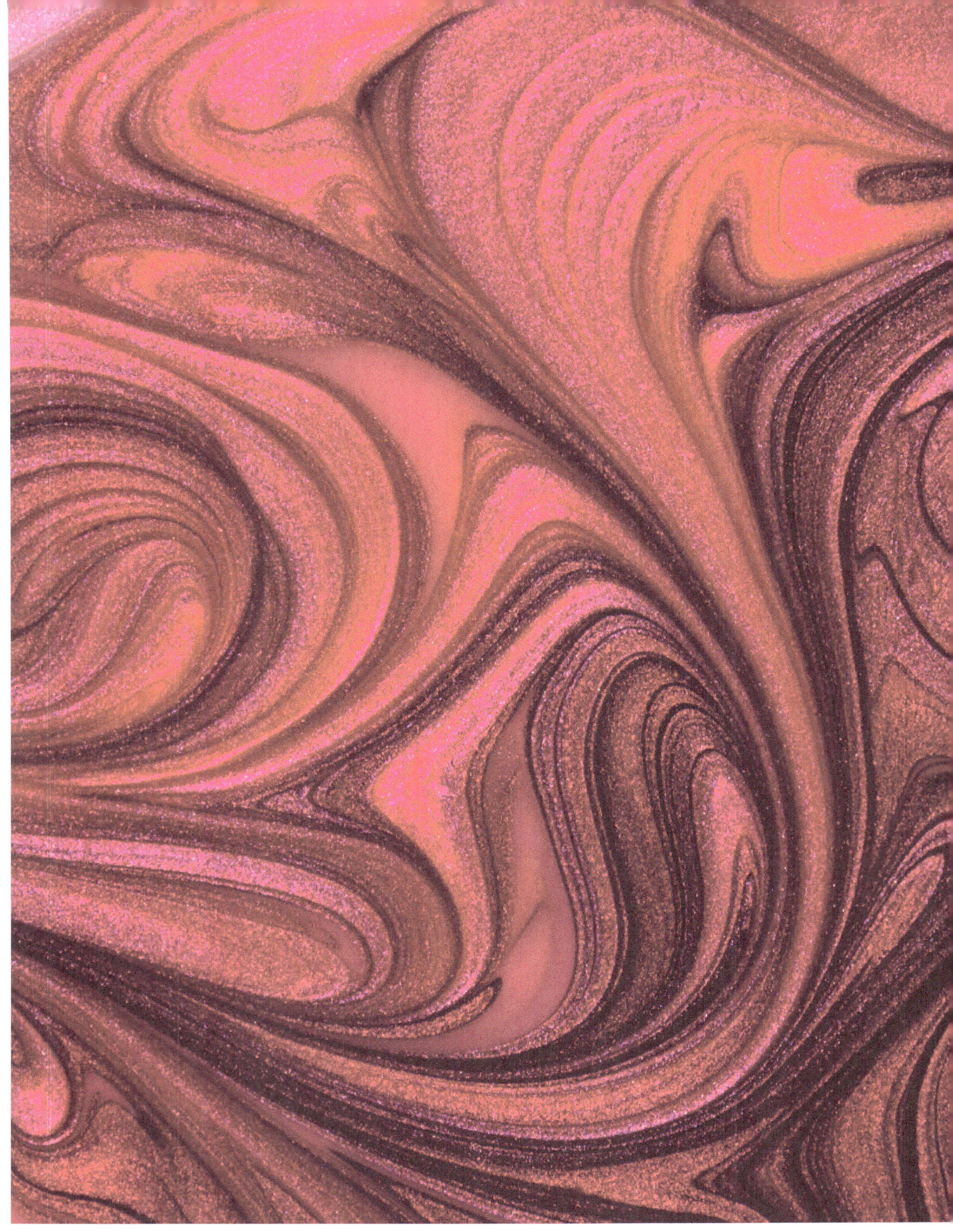

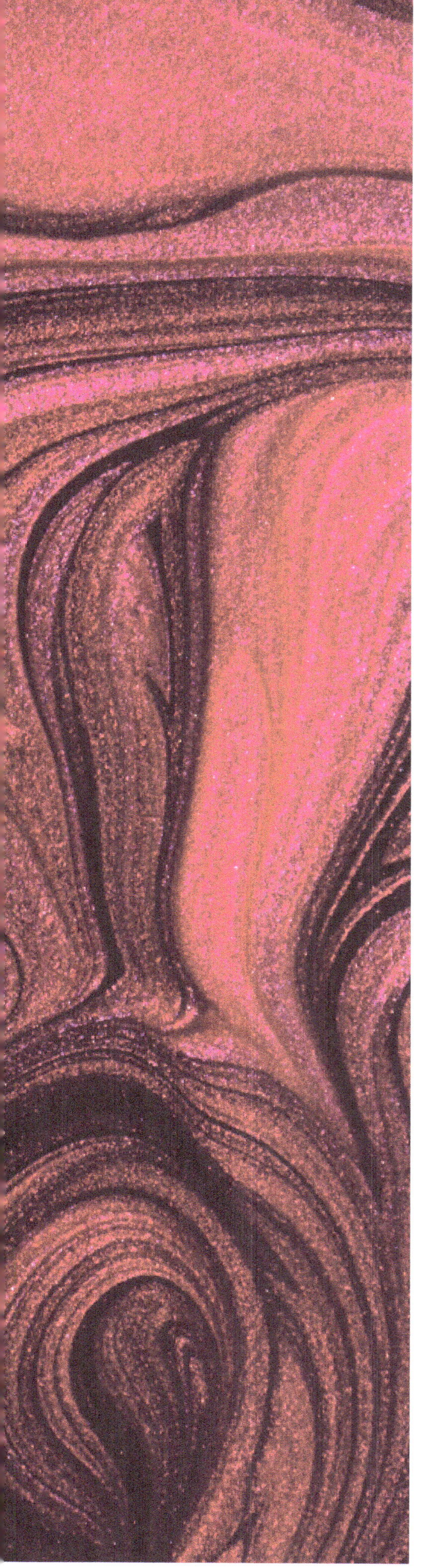

UTILIZE FREE FONTS

You will find numerous free font websites for one to start using!

Browse the web to get an inventory of free fonts for Cricut. You have to download the font and install it on your computer, and it will appear on your Cricut Design Space.

Regrettably, among the best fonts, Samantha Font isn't readily available freed from charge; however, confirm connection to find out where you can get it to get the absolute best price!

INSTALLING THEMES

After installing a ribbon to your computer, you would possibly want to sign in to Cricut Design Space before your font appears there. You would possibly even need to restart your PC so as for it to appear (mine wouldn't appear without restarting my PC).

For more information, read the ways to set up fonts from Cricut Design Space.

FIXING BLADES

Like that which Cricut blades wear out if the reductions are not any more so smooth and powerful, it's time for a shift. Other indicators that you need a brand-new blade to comprise:

• Tearing plastic or card
• Lifting or pulling vinyl off the backing sheet
• Not cutting all of the ways through (ensure your trimming setting is true too).

You can buy fresh blades from Amazon or see the Cricut Blade Guide for more purchasing choices.

WHENEVER YOUR FAVORITE LOSES ITS STICK

Cleaning your mat is one approach for slightly more life from your cutting mat. However, if it's beyond this, and you haven't purchased a brand-new cutting mat still, you can tape off your plastic or card to keep it in position.
You do not have to tape over an area. Ultimately, a couple of sides should perform the job. Even a moderate tack painters' tape is right for this undertaking and ought to not harm your cardstock.

VARIOUS BLADES FOR VARIOUS MATERIALS

Some folks swear by using different Blades for cutting every substance.
For example, using one blade that you use for cardstock, and yet one more that you merely use for the vinyl. That is because a spread of stuff will wear or on your blades. Cutting plastic is easier on the blade compared to the cutting card.

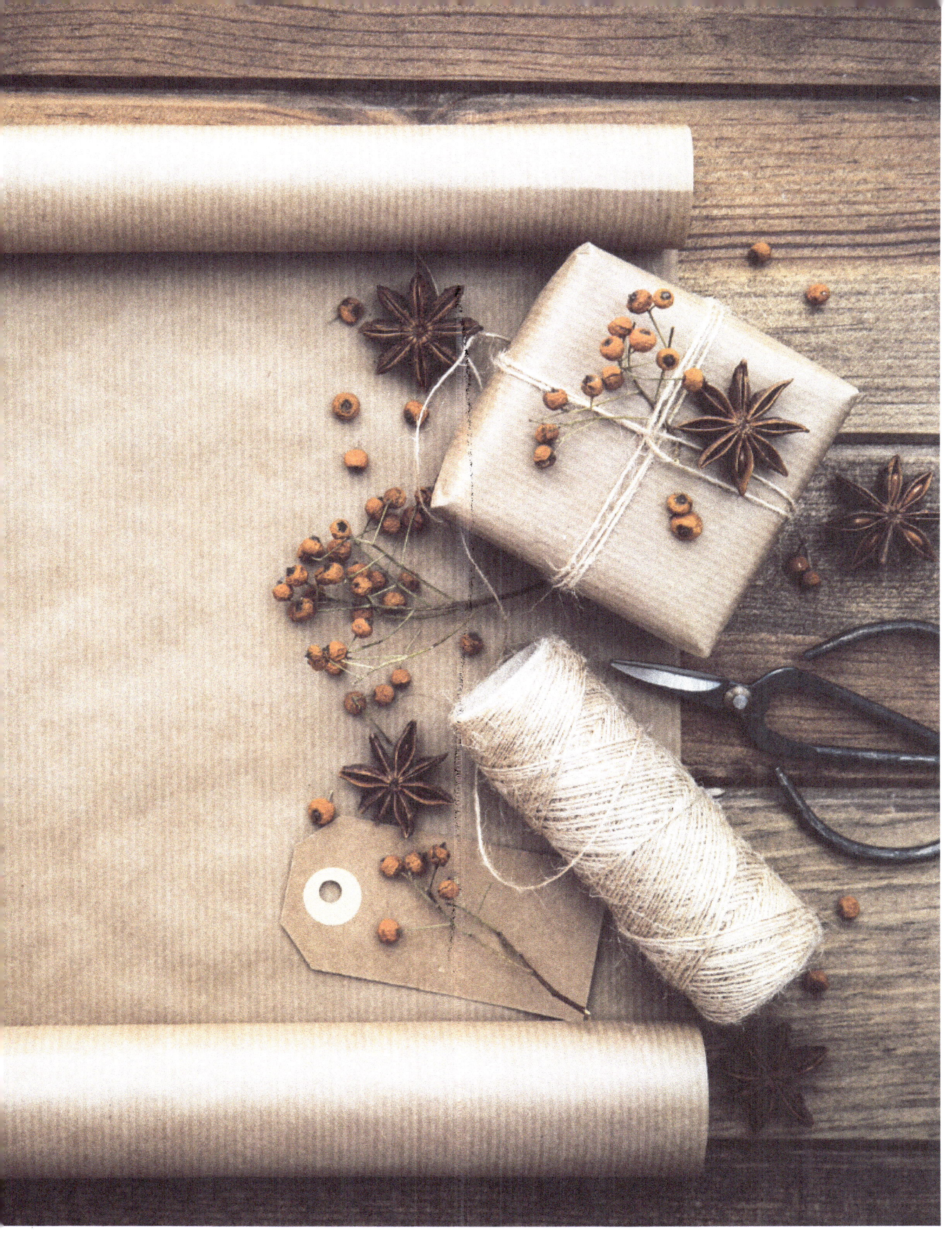

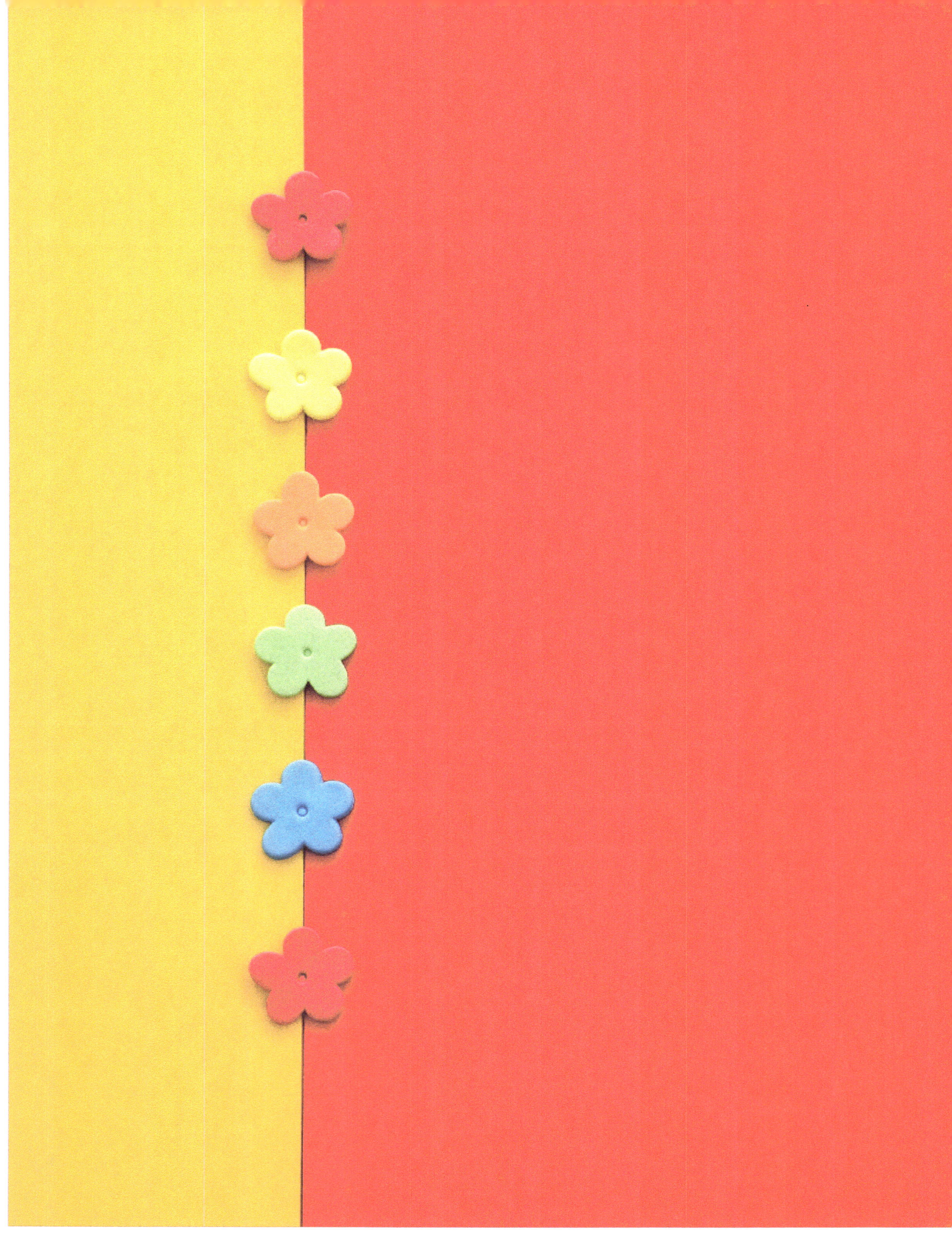

Having a committed blade to get vinyl means it will remain sharp and prepared, rather than having a blade to do all that immediately goes dull, then lifts your vinyl!

MIRROR YOUR PICTURES FOR HTV

If you are cutting heat transfer vinyl alongside your Cricut, you will have to mirror your design! Once you select 'Make It,' there is an option to mirror your layout (as seen below), and you will have to pick this choice for each mat!

SET HTV THE RIGHT WAY

You wil have to line your vinyl polished side down cn the outer mat to lower heat transport vinyl.
This way, the carrier sheet is beneath, alongside the dull plastic side is at the top. It is difficult to work out which side the carrier sheet is around, so remember polished side down, and you are going to be OK!

WEEDING BOXES

If you cre cutting a little or intricate layout or cutting an excellent deal of unique designs on one sheet of vinyl, it can help use weeding boxes. Use the square instrument in the Cricut design room to place a box around your layout and set both components together. Unlock the silhouette at the bottom left corner manipulate it in a rectangle.

This makes weeding easier than weeding several layouts simultaneously on the one sheet of vinyl and even more straightforward than attempting to watch where your layouts are and cutting them out individually using scissors.

DO NOT FORGET TO SET THE DIAL

This suggestion seems like a no-brainer; however, how often have I forgotten how to alter the material?

It is a simple thing to overlook -- Particularly when you have finally completed your layout and wish to get a clipping edge! The funny thing is that Cricut Design Space tells you precisely what substance the dial is put into if you are about to cut a layout -- but it isn't difficult to forget that also!

Save the error of cutting throughout to a cutting mat, or perhaps through your cardstock -- check your dialup!

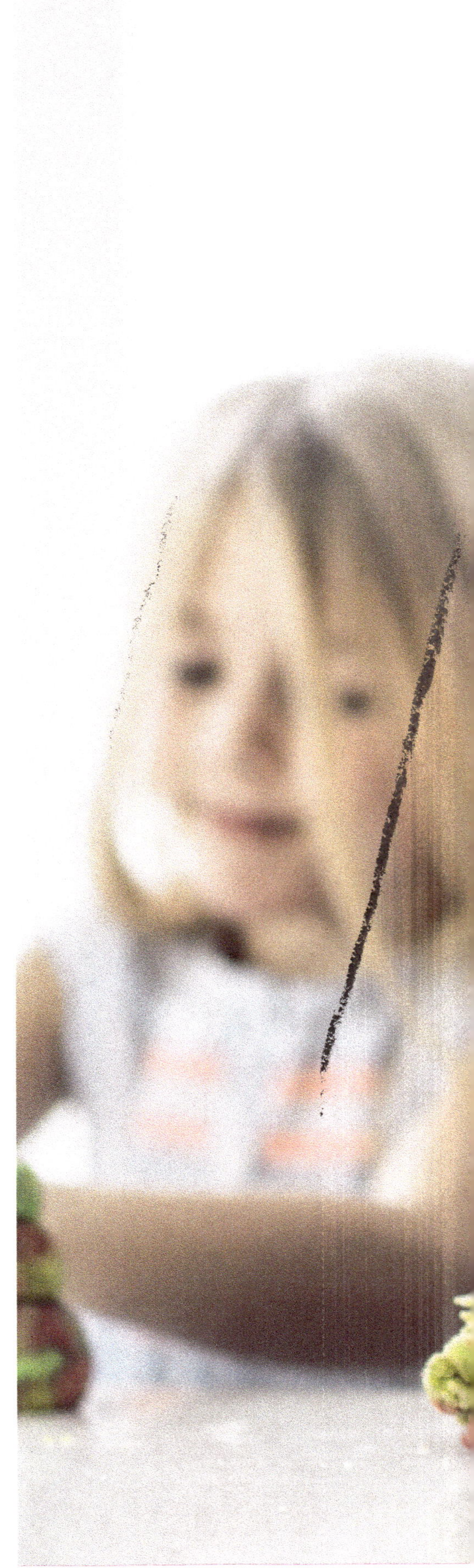

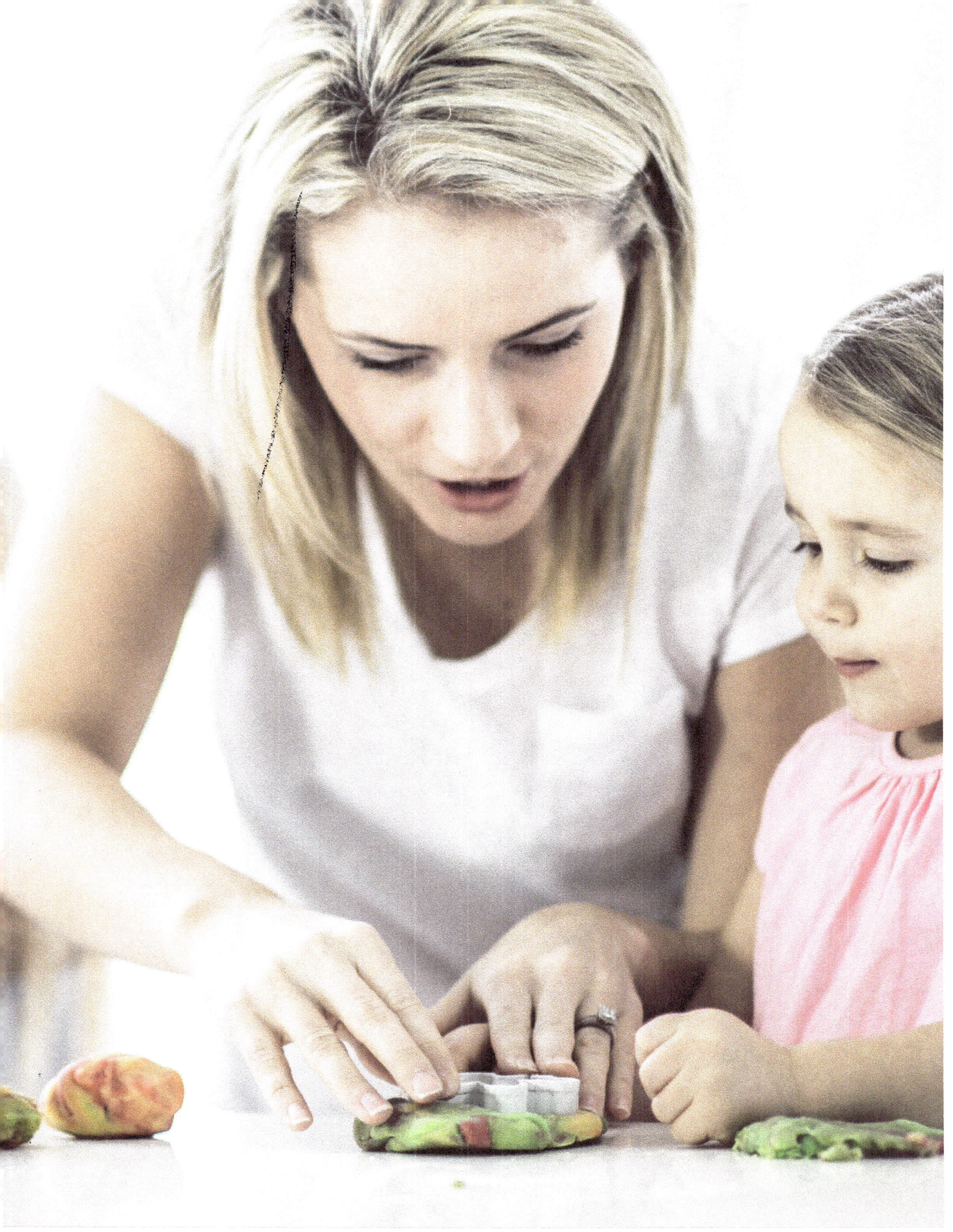

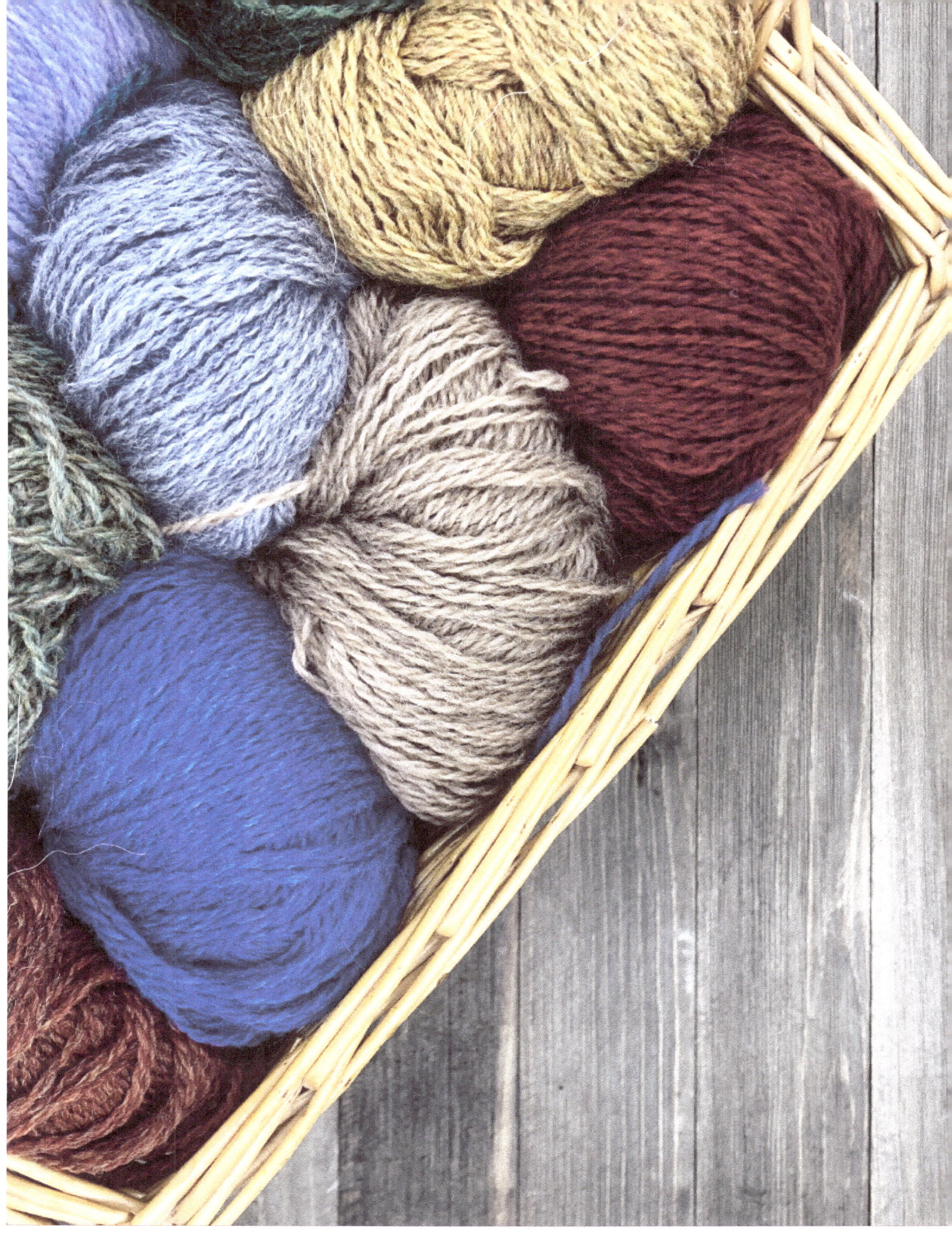

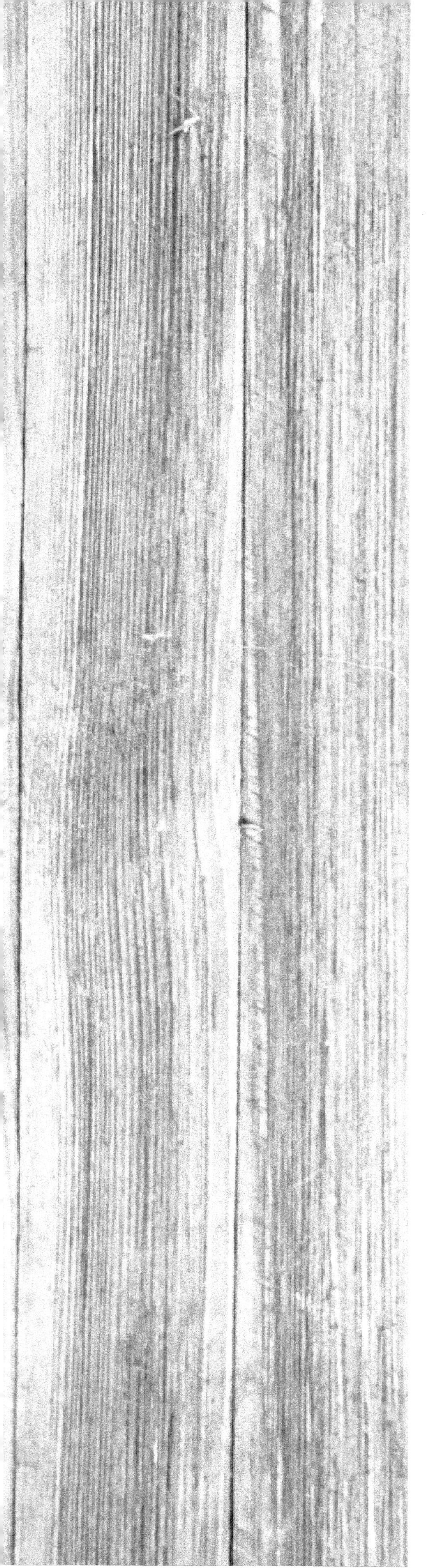

KEEP A SOURCE OF MATERIALS

If you'd wish to begin a project and you do not have the right tools. In these instances, we have been capable of working with no grading stylus, without the perfect pencil for the job, and with no profound cut blade. However, another hassle is if you'd wish to do a project and you have run out of glue, plastic, HTV, or cardstock!

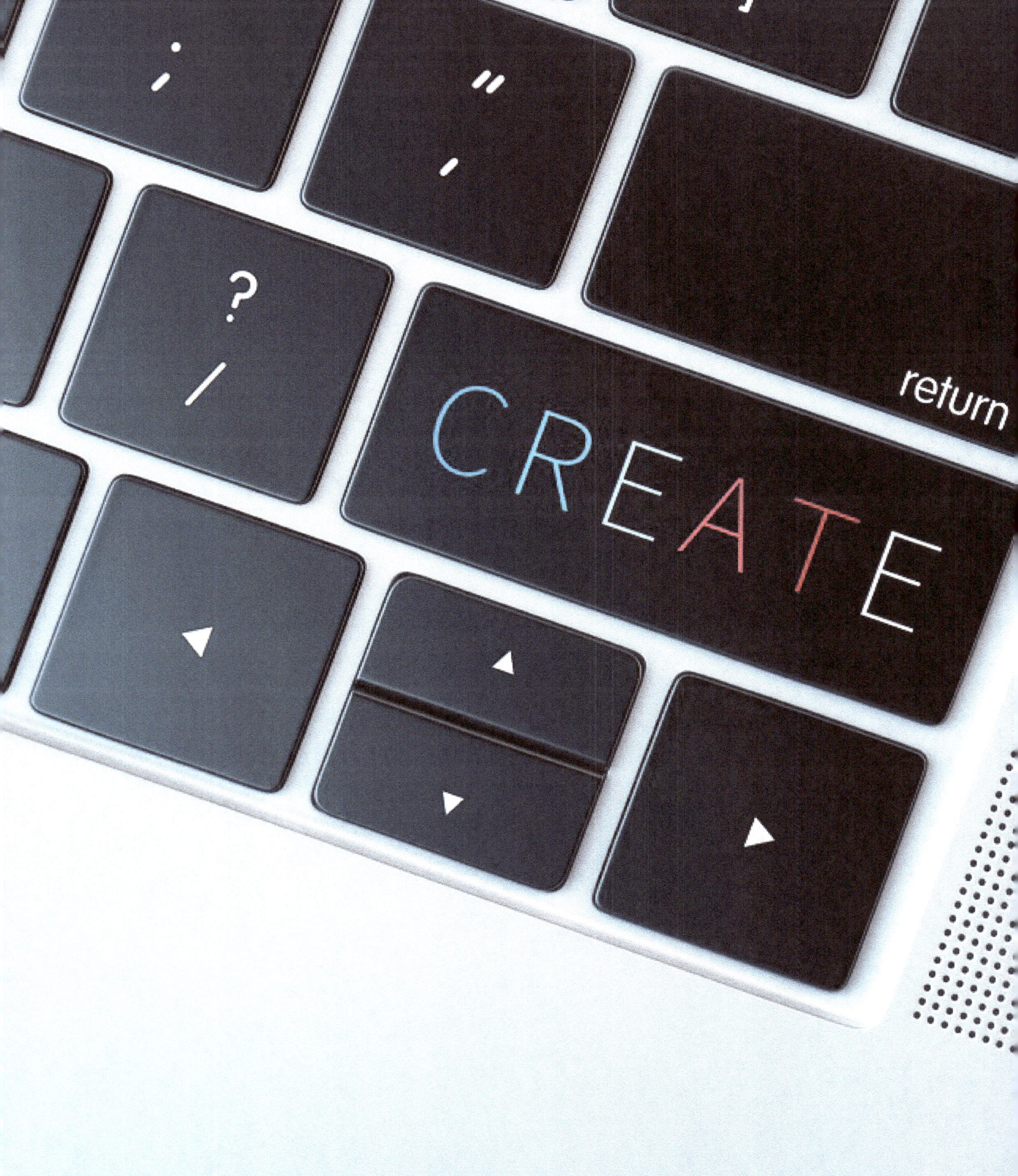

return
CREATE

Chapter 5
Best Websites with Free SVG Files

There are many websites where you can download and use free SVG files. It is effortless to download them and use them in your projects. These are readily available without any charges on the internet, so you can use them without worrying about their cost.

The weosite has different SVG categories like Books, Cars, Roads, Fashion, Digital Sketching, and much more. You just need to select the SVG file that you want and click on the download button. Then you will be able to see options like scale or pattern etc., choose one according to your requirement.

Mostly you will find a zip file with many images in it for the single SVG file, which will have different colors for every image in it and usually with a transparent background to combine it with any other image for making a pattern or something else.

Such files help make banners or something else where there should be multiple color options for the same shape of an object like a car or book cover etc.

There are websites where you can find SVG Files for your Cricut Projects and for making scrapbook pages.
There are certain websites where you need to register before downloading the files. But it is free of cost and straightforward to do so, then you can download as many SVG files as you want. The best thing about SVG files is that they are universal and can be used in operating systems like Linux, Microsoft Windows, Mac OS X, Android, etc. So you don't need to worry if your operating system supports this or not.

The main objective of SVG files is to make web pages more interactive by adding some animation in it or something else, and there are different websites where you can use these types of files for achieving this purpose like:

CSS Wizardry has a collection of free Cascading Style Sheets used on various websites with at-

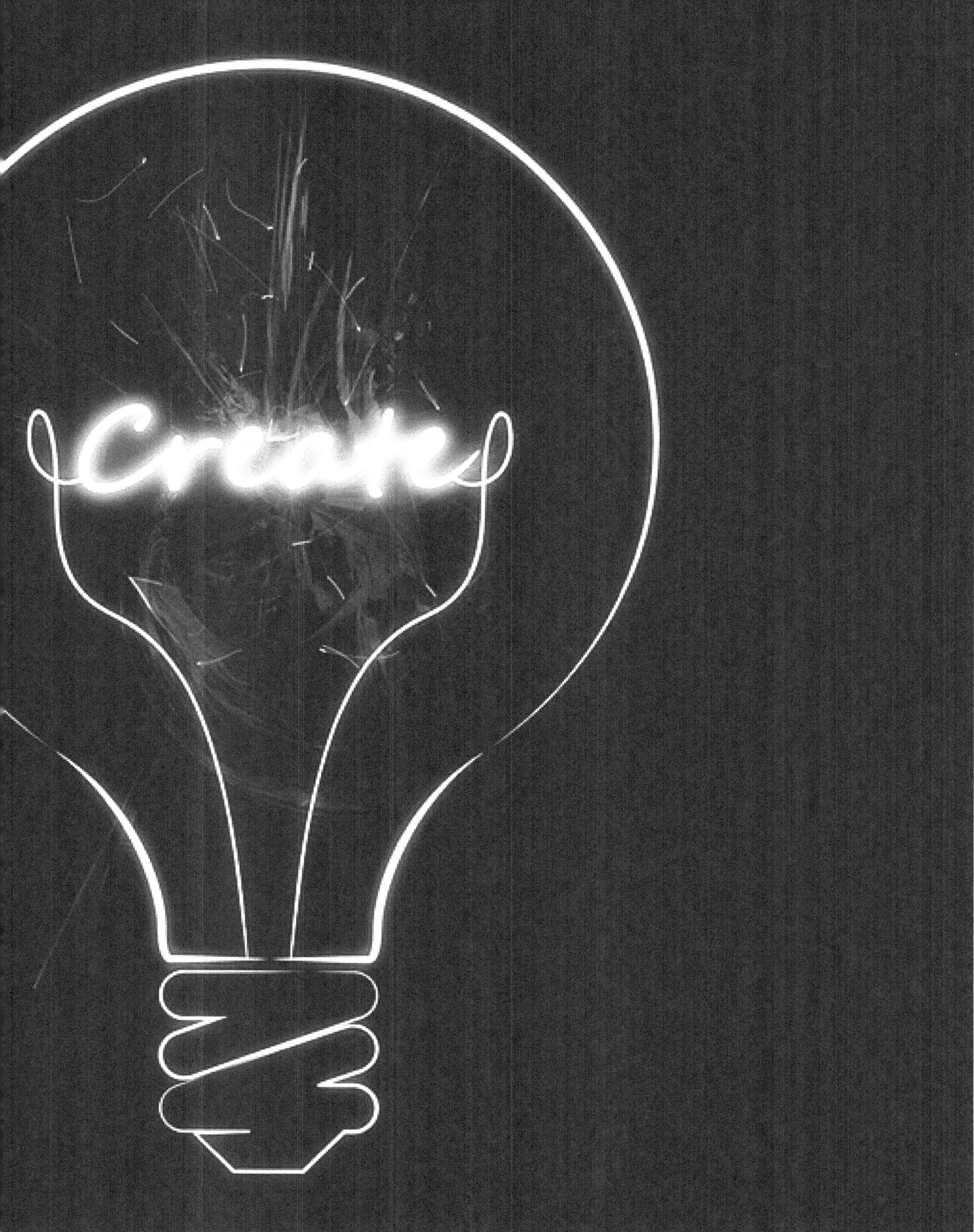

Create

Setting

tractive designs that may help designers create something new and unique according to their choice with these stylesheets.

This webste also provides a collection of tutorial videos for designers who want to learn about CSS3 animations and effects that can be used in web designing projects, including games.
Here are websites where you can find SVG Files for your Cricut Projects:

1.WWW.CRICUT.COM/

This website is a popular one where you can find almost anything for your Cricut and other personal projects

2. WWW.CUTTINGFILESCLUB.COM/FREE_STUFF.HTML

This website has a collection of free SVG File

3. WWW.FREE-SVG-FILES.COM/

Here you can find free SVG Files !

4.   WWW.SVGOOGLESLIDESHOWS.COM/

This website allows you to choose the type of files you want and download those you require.

5.   SVGWEBDESIGNERCONSULTING.COM/

This website allows us to select a file according to our requirement and download it in zip form along with its properties such as color display or transparent background etc. so that we can use them in any other project in our way according to our choice without worrying about their size or quality etc.

6.   WWW.DIGITALCRAFTMACHINE.COM/ FOR-THE-CRICUT-CUTTLEBUG-AND-OUTLINER

All these websites have the same purpose that is to provide free SVG files for your Cricut and other cutting machines even you are using a third-party extension (adds) like: "The Cricut Design Lab", "The Outliner", "Cuttlebug" and "Cinder".

7.   WWW.COOLSCRAPSBYMYDESIREAUSSIER.BLOG-SPOT. CO... -

This website contains a collection of personalized papers, prints, cards, etc., which can be used for

White feathers

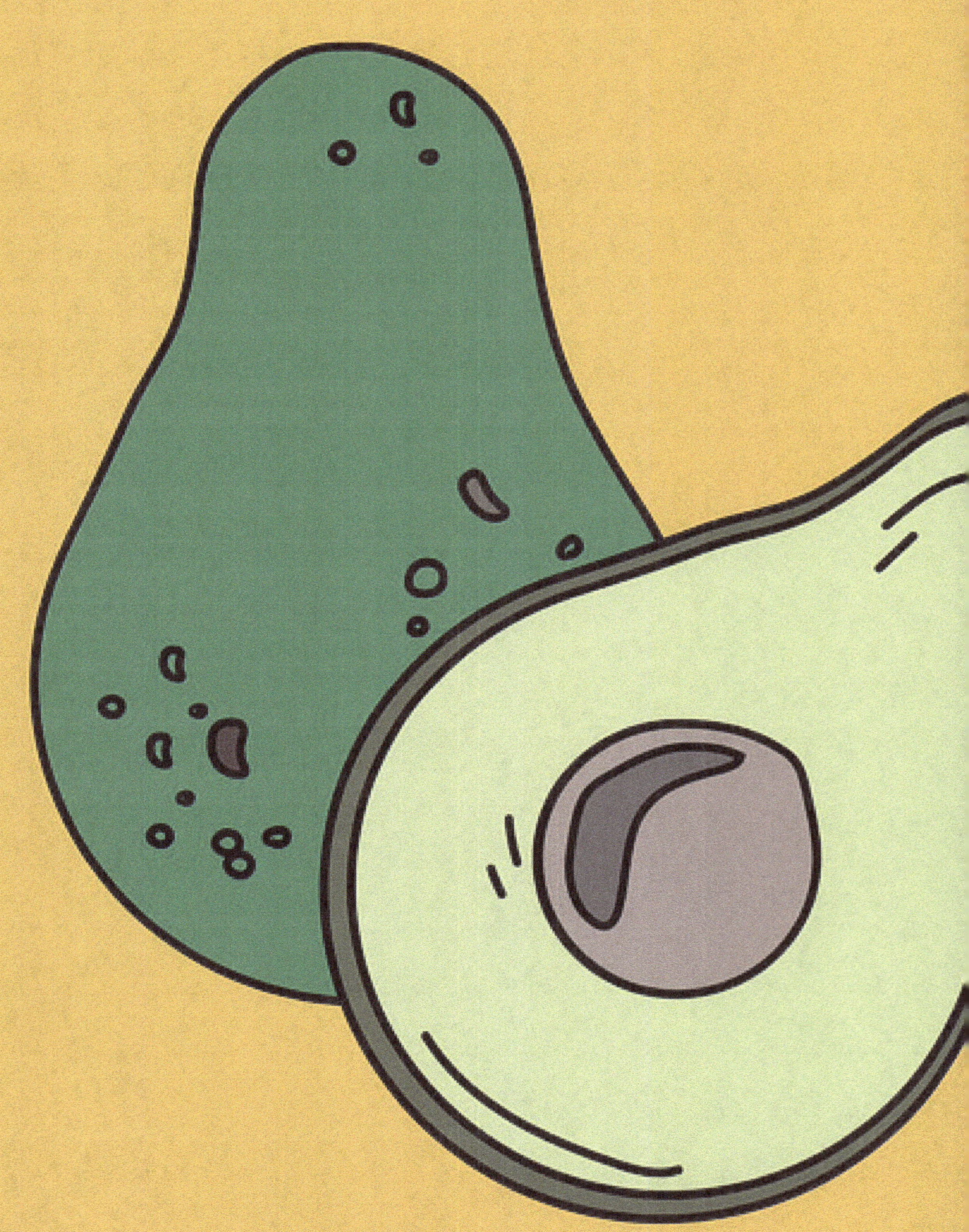

designing on Cricut and other machines.

8.   WWW.SVGCUTS.COM/

- This website has two options to download the files according to your choice, one is a zip download. and another one is a direct download by clicking on the file you require. Still, if you are using IE, you might face problems, but it is easy to fix this problem by changing your IE browser mode to "Internet Explorer 8 Compatible" or "IE7 Compatibility View".

9.   WWW.SCRAPINCUTS.COM/ -

Here, you have a variety of different SVG files like:
♥ Heart SVG Files ♥ Circle Cut Files ♥ SVG Tags ♥ Tag Cut File Set ♥ Christmas Ornaments ♥ Delicate Circles Cut File Pack ♥ Button Image Cut Files etc.,

10.   WWW.SVGCUTTLESCRAPPER.WORDPRESS.COM/

- Here, you will find the latest and best free SVG cut files for your personal use on Cricut, etc.

Chapter 6
Frequently Asked Questions

WHERE CAN I FIND IMAGES TO USE FOR MY PROJECT?

One of the great things with Cricut is that you can upload files from any source so long as you have the legal rights to use this image, as the space for Cricut Design and the ability to house so many different file types is fantastic. If you sell your designs, it is essential to use copyright-free images or purchase the images you include in your designs.

DO I NEED TO BUY ALL MY CRICUT FONTS?

Cricut Design Space can use fonts installed on your computer when you browse for your fonts. The fonts can be purchased or used for downloading via the Cricut Design Space with little to no problems. Across the Web, too, there is a range of resources for this.

Nevertheless, if you use a font, make sure you have a license to use the font for the reasons you want to use it! Fonts have copyrights, just like images, and can be limited to what you can do with them.

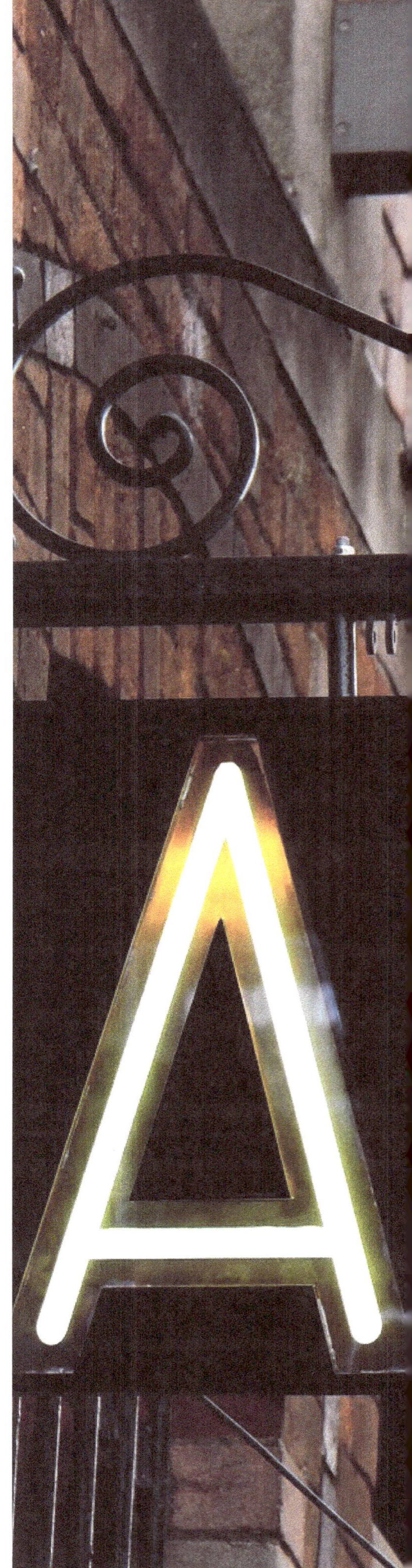

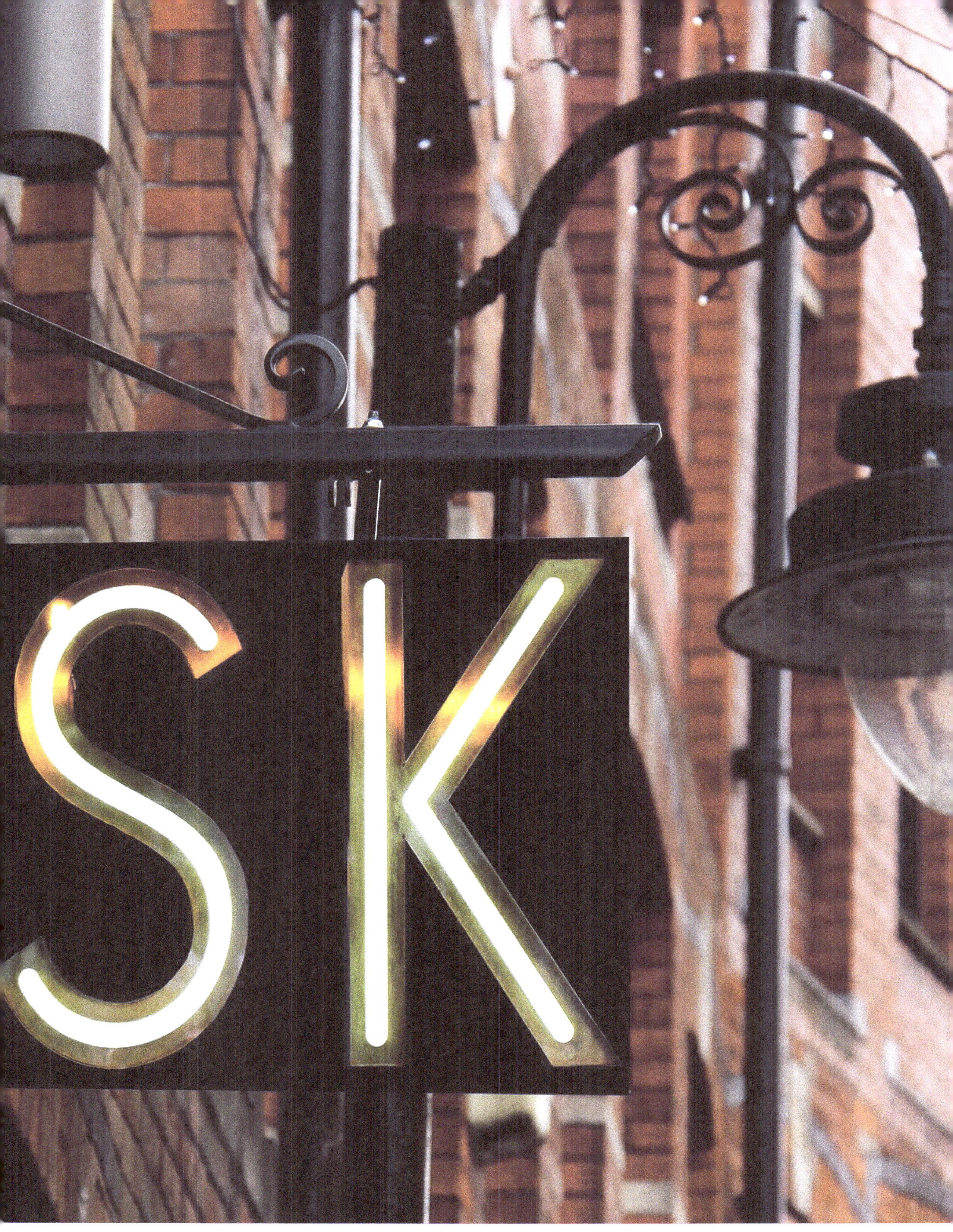
SK

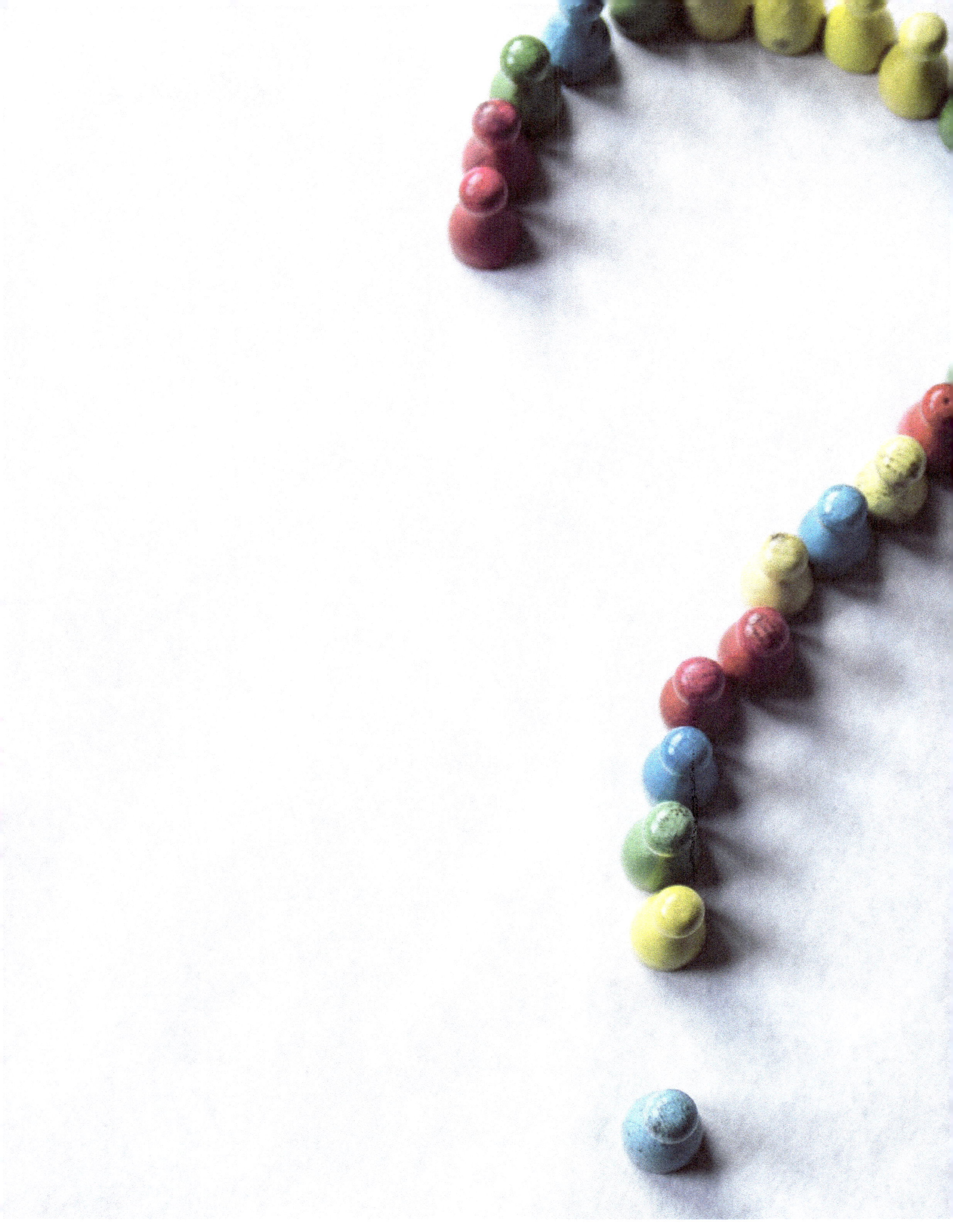

WHY DOES MY BLADE CUT MY SUPPORT SHEET?

It could be due to inappropriate seating on the packages blade, so move the package back, bring the blade into it again, load it up again and try again. It could also be because the content dial is not adjusted correctly. You can plunge the needle right through the whole material and the back if you cut anything very slim but have the dial set to cardstock.

WHY DON'T MY PICTURES APPEAR RIGHT ON MY MAT?

Once you press "Print it," it is likely that your print version doesn't look like anything in Design Space. When this happens, go back to Design Space, highlight all your photos, click "Team," then click "Attach," and all your project cutting needs will be kept right wherever they are.

HOW DO I USE DESIGN SPACE ON MY CHROMEBOOK?

Cricut's Design Space is unfortunately not currently designed for Chromebook OS compatibility. The application to download the plugin is a significant obstacle to the operating system, but that doesn't mean that there will be no compatibility shortly.

CAN I USE THE DESIGN SPACE ON MORE THAN ONE DEVICE?

Sure, all designs, components, fonts, transactions, and photos are accessible via any internet-connected device and your account credentials, thanks to the web-based and club-based features of Cricut. You can start a design during the day and then wrap it up once you're back in your crafting space from any device.

HOW MANY TIMES CAN I USE AN IMAGE PURCHASED IN THE DESIGN SPACE?

Any design asset or feature you purchase from the design space will be yours to use as much as you like when you have an active Cricut Design Space account. Feel free to cut as many designs as you want from your purchased images.

CAN I DEACTIVATE OR SWITCH THE DESIGN SPACE GRID?

Indeed, you can switch grid lines from the design room. Open the Accord menu (three lines stacked at the top left) and select Settings on a

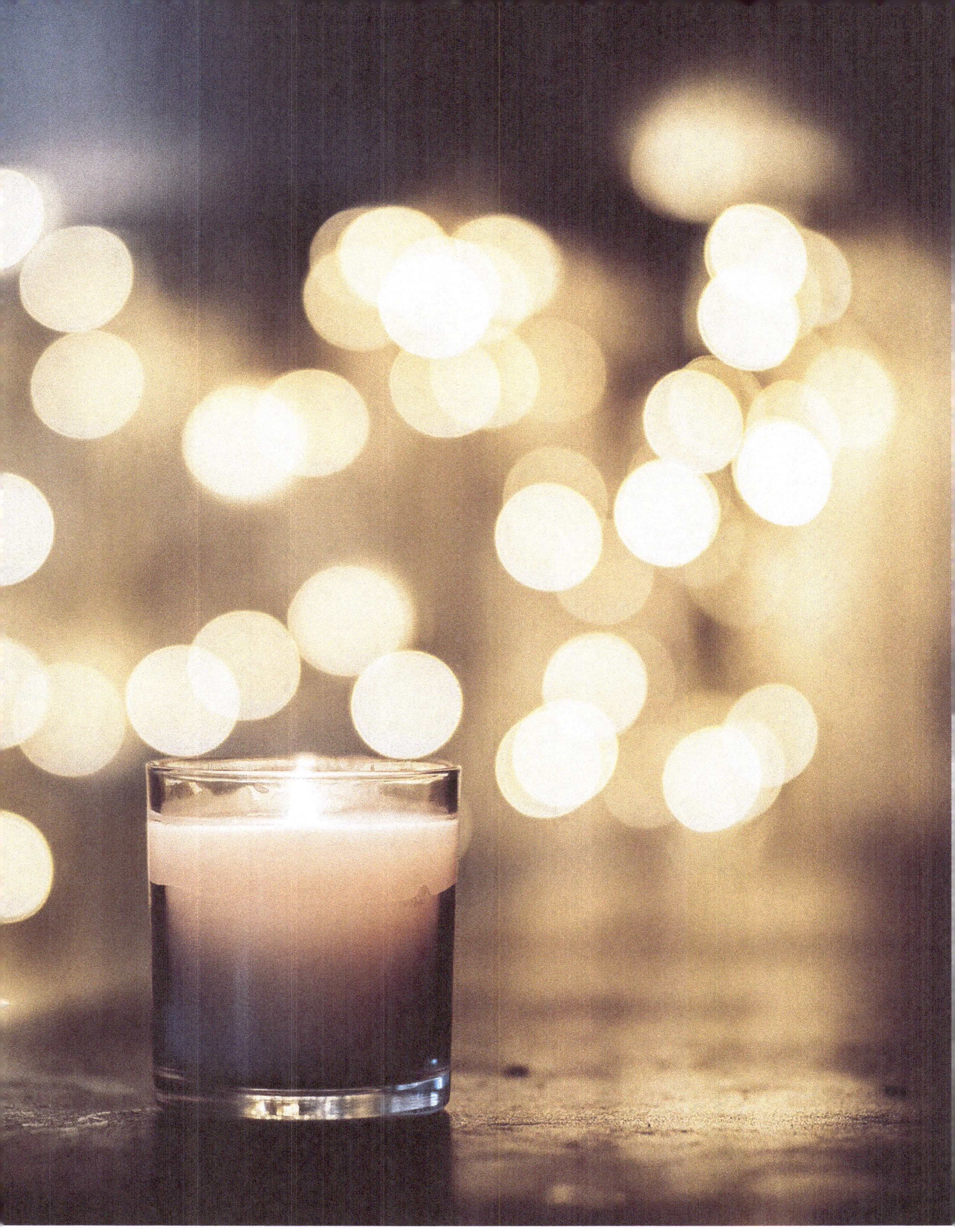

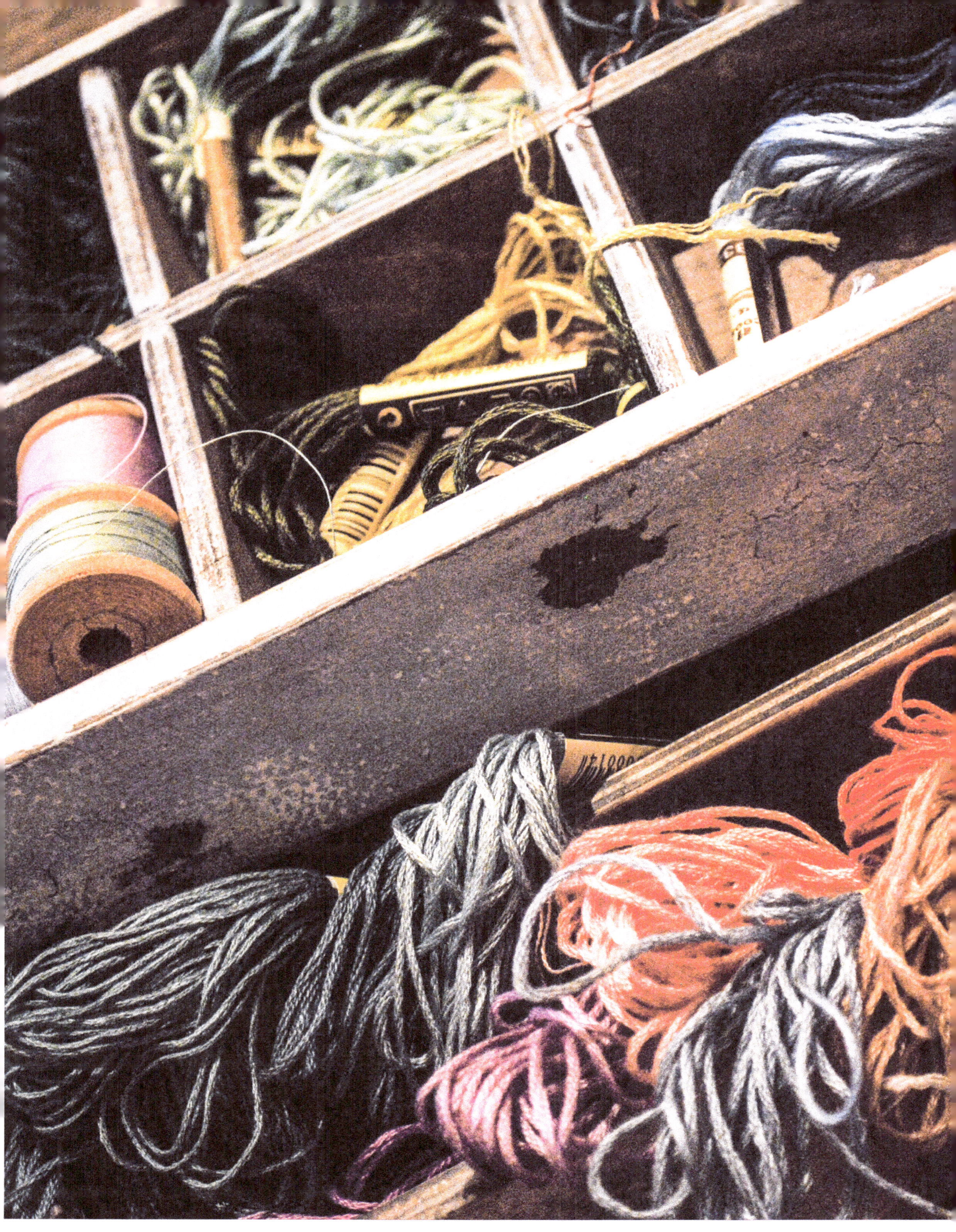

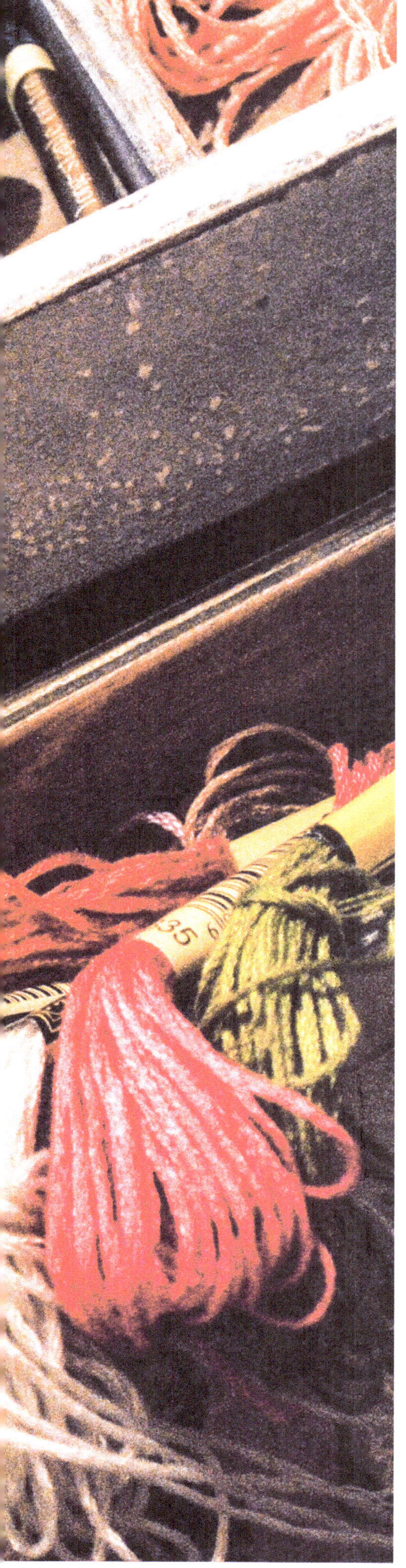

Windows / Mac device. The Canvas Grid choices are available, and you can select your preference. You can also see shortcuts in the settings menu. Select the keyboard shortcut to turn off and on grid lines.

HOW DO I CONVERT TO METRIC UNITS?

To switch to centimeters from inches on a laptop or desktop, open the Account menu; you'll see three stacked lines in the upper left corner, then select Settings. You'll see the options to select inches or centimeters.

WHAT EXACTLY IS SNAPMAT?

SnapMat is an iOS-exclusive feature that lets you get a virtual preview of what you are making. This gives you the ability to align your designs in Design Space to fit perfectly with what you put on your mat. This functionality allows you to place images and text over your mat's snapshot so that you can see exactly how your layout should be in the design space.

WHAT ARE THE BENEFITS OF USING SNAPMAT?

SnapMat gives you the certainty that your images will be placed in when you send your design to cut through your Cricut. It will show you where your pictures are drawn, how cuts are made, and how the text lines up. With SnapMat, you can tell your Cricut to cut a specific piece of a pattern that you've stuck on your mat, write in specific stationery areas, gift tags, envelopes, or cards, and you can get the most out of your scraps and spare materials left from past projects.

CAN I INCLUDE MULTIPLE SNAPMAT MATS AT ONE TIME?

SnapMat can snap one mat at a time. If you want to snap multiple mats, you can do so individually and work that way through your designs. This ensures that each mat is shot correctly and that each one is done accurately.

WHAT'S CRICUT DESIGN SPACE OFFLINE MODE?

This feature is available exclusively through the iOS platform. This feature allows you to download your items for later use in an offline environment. This is ideal if you plan to work on your designs for a prolonged time in a space

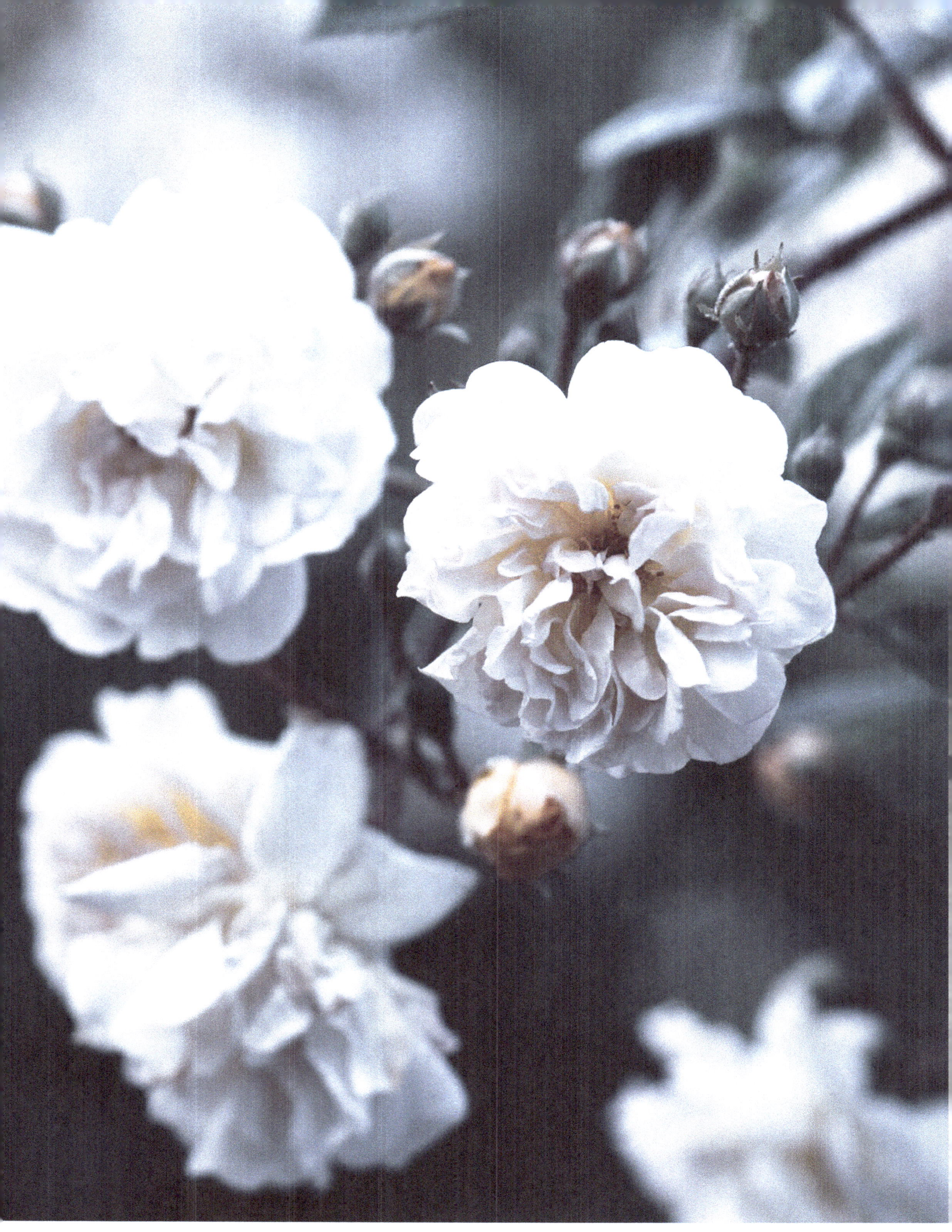

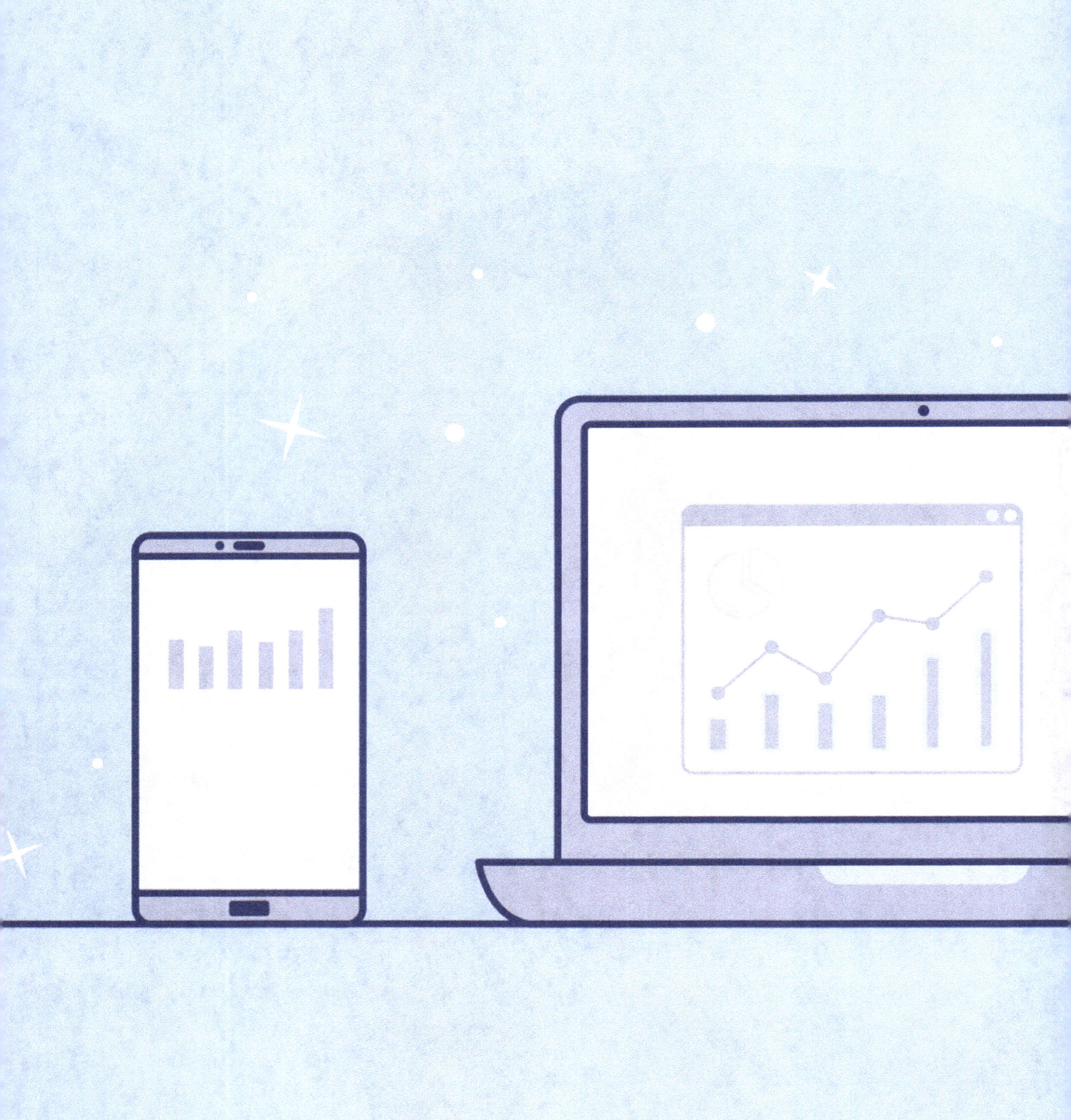

that doesn't have an active internet connection. You can still work on your designs during that time without worrying about losing those creative thoughts.

WHAT IS AVAILABLE FOR OFFLINE DOWNLOAD?

You can download any element or asset that you own or have purchased rights through Cricut Design Space for offline use. This includes images you uploaded from other devices, images, or assets obtained through active membership in Cricut Access. It is up to you to pick what assets you want to make available for offline use.

HOW DO I SAVE PROJECTS THAT ALLOW ME TO USE THEM OFFLINE?

This step can only be accomplished with an active internet connection, so be sure to download before going offline. Open a project that you want to save for use offline and select the option "Save As." Select the option "Save to this iPad / iPhone," which will allow you to use the project without any connection later.

HOW DO I SAVE OFFLINE CHANGES TO MY PROJECTS?

Suppose you are going to work on a project in offline mode. In that case, tap "Save," and the file you saved to your device will be updated automatically without having to reselect the option "Save to this iPad / iPhone" if there is no internet connection.

Can I Download Images for Subsequent Offline Use?

You may download images to your device later, offline use, while you have an active internet connection. To do so, open the "Images" screen, select an image, and tap "Download." When this is done, the image label will indicate, and the image will be available immediately, irrespective of an available internet connection.

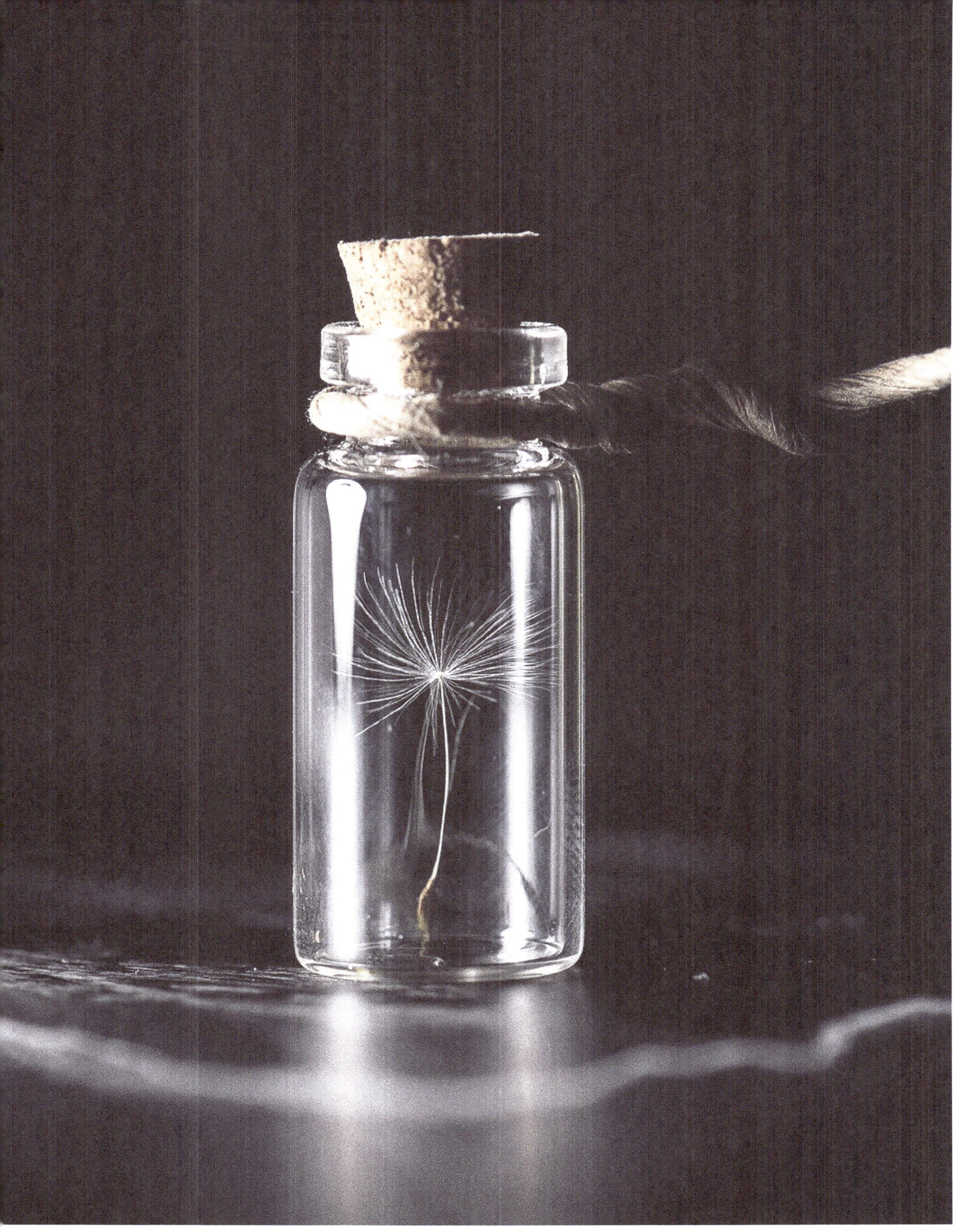

Conclusion

It is no longer news that digital die-cutting units are incredibly restrictive for craft enthusiasts and people who love the Cricut die-cutting system.

They mostly allow users to cut a small number of fonts, and they are not cheap at all.

Thankfully, a few programs out there have managed to open Cricut to enable them to cut designs, TrueType fonts created by users, and many more.

Below is a list of the best third-party software to use with Cricut.

Make the Cut

This is an excellent third-party Cricut Design software that comes with simple but highly effective design features, e.g., it packs quick lattice tools, and it can convert raster images into vectors for cutting. The program has been around for some time. Some of the most outstanding features of the tool include:

·It comes with advanced editing tools, and it is relatively easy to use (even for a newbie) because the user interface is effortless to learn.

·The software works with many file formats, and it also uses TrueType fonts.

·The software comes with a pixel trace tool that allows users to take and convert raster graphics into vector paths for cutting.

·For those that are interested, Make the Cut works with Gazelle, Craft ROBO, Wishblade, and Silhouette.

·Some other features include the fact that users can import the following: WPC, GSD, PS, AI9, EPS, OTF, TTF, SCUT, or PDF files and can also export shapes in SVG, Ai, EPS, PNG, and JPG formats.

Make the Cut is a user-friendly and flexible Cricut-related software that adds more utility to the digital die-cutting machine that is usually limited in usage and application.

Sure, Cuts A Lot

The Sure Cuts A Lot of software gives users complete control of their designs without the cartridges' restrictions featured in Cricut DesignStudio.

Users must install a firmware update to their Cricut die-cutting machine; however, they can do this for free by downloading the trial version of DesignStudio. It is a straightforward task to perform.

Some of the features of the Sure Cuts A Lot software include:

·It allows users to use the OpenType and TrueType fonts.

It is the one and only Cricut Design tool available that comes with freestyle drawing tools.

·It allows users to create unique designs with basic drawing and editing tools.

·The program works with Silhouette, Craft ROBO, and Wishblade die-cutting machines.

·It is specifically designed to open up all of Cricut's cutting features and abilities.

·It allows users to edit the individual nodes that make up the path.

·It comes with an auto trace feature that converts raster graphics into vector images.

·The programs have about 200 built-in shapes and other exciting features.

·It allows users to import different file formats, including PDF, SVG, AI, EPS, and WPC. The pro version allows users to import DXF and PLT.

·It allows users to select styles, including Blackout and Shadow, to quickly change shapes and letters with just a few clicks of the mouse.

·It allows users to use advanced features such as layers, grouping, and the weld tool to make the most out of their designs.

To download and get the complete set of Sure Cuts A Lot of features, you can check their website. The Sure Cuts A Lot program doesn't come with fonts; it only allows users to use the already on their computers.

Getting more fonts to your computer isn't a big deal because thousands of fonts are out there. Besides, you don't have to buy any special cartridges to get more fonts to your system.

Cricut DesignStudio

Cricut DesignStudio, a product of ProvoCraft, allows users to connect Cricut to a personal computer to do much more with Cricut fonts and shapes.

For those that don't know, Provo Craft is the same company that manufactures Cricut die-cutting machines. With the aid of various tools, this Cricut software allows users to adjust fonts and shapes.

Some of the best features of the software include:

·Users will be able to weld, flip, and rotate easily.

Users have the option of previewing and creating designs with different images from the Cricut library.

·Users will have to purchase a cartridge to cut.

·The software comes with a high level of customization to the Cricut library, and the extra features are beneficial.

·People who use this software are still limited to the same shapes and fonts from the cartridges they own but bearing in mind the tools packed in the program, which is not an issue.

The program remains a perfect option to use alongside your Cricut, and you'll be able to get the best out of its features. To know more about the software, go to their official website.

Inkscape

Inkscape is an open-source graphics editor for Windows and other operating systems. It is a professional program that costs absolutely nothing.

Users can use the program and Cricut to create and edit vector graphics such as illustrations, diagrams, line arts, logos, elaborate paintings, and much more.

Below are some of the features that come with the software:

It can be used to render primitive text and vector shapes.

·It supports embedding and optional tracing of raster graphics.

·The objects can be filled with solid colors, patterns, radial, linear color gradients, and others; their borders can be stroked with adjustable transparency.

·The program can be used to create vector graphics from multiple raster sources and pictures.

·Shapes created can be manipulated easily with different transformations: moving, rotating, scaling, and skewing.

There are many more features present in this powerful software, and the easiest way to get acquainted with them all is to visit Inkscape's official website.

To maximize the use of your Cricut machine, you should consider using these excellent software applications that are compatible with Windows systems.

For the best experience possible, you should pair them up with some 2D digital pixel art tools or with some photo editors.

Depending on what you choose to do, you will quickly take control of your creativity and use Cricut Design Space the way you've always dreamt of.

Thank you !!